THE GOOD, THE BAD & THE BEAUTIFUL

Stephanie Parker

ISBN: 979-8-9873095-5-1

Dedication

To Judy,
the beautiful in our story.
Your light shines where there was once only darkness.
Your joy is a miracle.
Thank you for letting your story be told.

To my mother,
who stood in the gap when we were unraveling.
You saved our family in ways no one else could.
I will never stop being grateful.

To every adoptive parent,
especially the ones hanging on by a thread,
This is for the sleepless nights, the silent grief, the invisible battles.
For the love you keep giving, even when it isn't returned.
You are not failing.
You are not alone.
May these pages offer you truth, solidarity, and a little bit of
strength for tomorrow.

1

I still remember the first day I saw Manny, Gio, and Judy. Manny and Gio came to us first, carrying nothing but a plastic bag with a few items of clothing and eyes far too old for their age, filled with fear. We found out later that they had a sister, Judy. No one in the entire city was willing to take three children. We had planned to adopt only one child, but agreed to take the two boys. When we learned they had a sister they had been separated from, and that she was all alone, we agreed to take all three so they could be together.

My life took a detour I never could have imagined. We felt a deep calling to adopt the three children from the foster care system, ages six, four, and two. When we welcomed them into our home, we were not told of the horrific abuse they had endured. We were told only that there had been minor neglect due to their mother's alcohol use. The horrific stories of their past came out gradually over the years, and only after the adoption was finalized.

Because we didn't know what they had endured, we were completely unprepared, both to help them heal and to protect our other children from the fallout of that trauma.

This is the story of each of my adopted children's journey to adulthood in our home. Some of the stories are heartwarming. Many are heartbreaking. This is not a cautionary tale. It is a call for preparedness, compassion, and better support for families stepping into the world of trauma-informed adoption. Whether you want to understand what adoptive families go through out of curiosity, or whether you're considering adopting yourself, being informed is pivotal when caring for children who come from difficult circumstances.

One of my greatest regrets is that we didn't receive the trauma-informed training we so desperately needed. If I had known what could happen: the good, the bad, and the beautiful, I believe I could have faced the curveballs with more readiness and resilience.

Every adoption story is unique. While this book focuses primarily on the intense challenges of adopting older children, especially those with significant early trauma, I want to acknowledge that infant adoption carries its own complexities.

Some infants are adopted into stable, nurturing homes and thrive with fewer visible emotional wounds. Others experience deep, lasting impacts from early loss, separation, and prenatal drug & alcohol exposure. I've seen both.

This book doesn't represent every adoptive journey, especially not those that begin in infancy, but it does seek to tell the truth about the kind of adoption stories we often avoid talking about. If your experience looks different, that doesn't make either of our stories more or less valid; it just makes them different. And adoption is filled with both kinds.

Whether considering infant adoption or older child adoption, my hope is not to scare you, but to help you walk into adoption with truth as your guide.

Each chapter in this book focuses on one of the adopted children: Manny, Gio, or Judy. It shares the details of their story, some joyful and some heartbreaking, all real. You'll walk through the milestones, the meltdowns, the healing, and the hope.

While our journey was marked by pain, it also brought resilience, grace, and an understanding of love I never knew existed. If you're considering adopting older children, please don't shy away from it. It is needed. But be informed and be ready for the challenges that come with it. Whether you are simply curious or seriously considering adoption, my hope is that this book gives you the insight I so desperately needed.

This is my story, focused on trauma-impacted, older-child domestic adoption. Adoption, especially of children from trauma, is not for the faint of heart. But with understanding, support, and preparation, it is an extraordinary journey of healing and transformation.

While this book delves into the complexities and challenges often associated with adopting older children, it's essential to recognize that adoption experiences are diverse. Many families who adopt infants encounter their own unique joys and trials. This narrative aims to shed light on one facet of adoption, not to generalize all experiences.

Thank you for walking this road with me. You are stepping into sacred, hard, beautiful work. My hope is that our story helps you step into it with open eyes and a full heart.

2

I'm starting with stories of Manny, the child I couldn't save because his role in our family shows just how devastating adoption can be when things go wrong. Some stories need to be brought into the light, even when they're hard to tell. Not many adoption stories are as dark as Manny's, but his reveals the hardest side of adoption. It doesn't always go this way, but if you're considering adoption, you need to know the good, the bad, and the beautiful.

Manny came to us at six years old, already carrying a weight no child should bear. His mother, trapped in prostitution, had sold him more than once. When she wasn't able to prostitute herself, she would sell Manny to help pay for her addiction to alcohol and drugs.

On many days, he survived on nothing but stale crackers and sips of leftover beer from half-empty bottles that littered the living room floor. He didn't drink it to get drunk; he drank it because he was thirsty, and the tap water had long since turned brown.

Twice, Manny escaped house fires; fires he accidentally started while trying to cook for himself. His mother would be passed out on the couch, lost in a haze of drugs and alcohol, unreachable. And so the responsibility fell to him. He was just a little boy, maybe five or six, climbing up onto counters to reach pots, turning knobs on the stove, guessing his way through tasks no child should be left to handle.

The flames rose quickly, once from oil spattering onto a hot burner, another time from a dishtowel left too close to the heat. Both times, panic surged through him. He didn't dare wake his mother. He knew better. The punishment for interrupting her sleep was often worse than the danger itself. But survival screamed louder than fear. He had to get out.

Somehow, she woke. Whether from the smoke or the noise, she came to and managed to put the fire out. Then she turned on him. The rage wasn't about the fire; it was about the inconvenience, the mess, the shame. He was beaten. Not comforted. Not reassured. Just punished, because he'd needed something she couldn't give: safety.

And that's just one story we know.

There are likely so many more we don't. Manny rarely spoke of his early years. When he did, it was in clipped phrases, vague hints. But his silence told its own story. We saw it in the scars on his body. We saw it in the way he flinched when someone reached too quickly for a hug or dropped a spoon too loudly. For years, his body lived on high alert. Even in rest, his shoulders were never fully relaxed.

His birth mother was deeply unstable. One time, in a drug-fueled rage, she chased a man through the house with a butcher's knife. Manny witnessed it all. Sometimes he was the target; other times, the helpless bystander. Abuse wasn't an episode for him; it was the atmosphere of his childhood. He breathed it in like secondhand smoke.

He learned early that love could turn violent, that safety was fragile, and that adults were unpredictable. By the time he came to us, he wasn't looking for love. He was looking for escape.

And those are just the parts I know. Much of his early trauma remains a mystery locked away in silence. I learned these stories only after the adoption was finalized and when I did, it shattered the narrative I had clung to, the one where love alone would be enough to erase the past.

The state didn't tell us. Maybe they didn't know. Or maybe they did, and feared no one would take him if they understood the full depth of his past. They were probably right. If I knew one of our adopted children had been human trafficked and the severity of his abuse, It might have made me reevaluate our decision before it was permanent.

* * *

I wish this had been an Anne of Green Gables story where adoption brings rescue, and a child blooms in the warmth of love and safety. I hoped that bringing Manny into our family would be his turning point. That he would feel chosen, safe, and finally able to heal.

What followed wasn't healing; it was chaos, heartbreak, and an unraveling I never saw coming.

Even with us, his world stayed haunted by something far darker: rage, mistrust, and pain that refused to loosen its grip.

Those first days with Manny were strangely quiet. He wasn't difficult, not in the way I expected a traumatized child to be. He didn't scream or throw tantrums. He just... didn't feel present. His face was mostly expressionless, his eyes flat. He didn't cry, didn't laugh, didn't show much at all.

At the time, I thought that was normal trauma in a child. I assumed he was shut down, and that safety and love would slowly bring him out. But looking back, those were warning signs I didn't know how to read.

His play was strange: stilted and immature, often repetitive, like he was stuck in toddlerhood. From the beginning, I sensed something was off intellectually, too. He couldn't form full sentences, had trouble understanding basic instructions, and his comprehension lagged far behind.

His face looked different; something I couldn't quite name at the time. Now I recognize the facial features of fetal alcohol syndrome. Later, testing confirmed what I had sensed all along: an IQ of 79, just below the threshold of what's considered average. His delays weren't just from trauma. They were neurological, permanent. But in those early days, I didn't know any of that. I still believed he would catch up. I still believed love would be enough.

Manny's cognitive delays were not what made him so difficult. I've known many children and adults with intellectual disabilities, and none of them made the kinds of choices Manny did. His low IQ was just one layer in a much more tangled story. It was one more element that made parenting him so disorienting. It complicated everything. He couldn't grasp cause and effect, couldn't retain boundaries, and often didn't seem to understand why his actions had consequences.

But his delays alone didn't explain the defiance, the cruelty, or the darkness that began to show itself over time. Those things came from somewhere deeper; something that love couldn't reach. Looking back, the delays weren't the root of the behavior, but they certainly made it harder to navigate.

It's one thing to deal with defiance from a child who can understand correction. It's another thing entirely when the child seems locked in a fog you can't break through, no matter how hard you try.

Looking back, the biggest warning sign I missed, the one I now realize should have stopped me in my tracks, was Manny's lack of empathy. That first year, he didn't get into much trouble himself. He kept his head down, played along, and masked whatever darkness was hiding underneath. But there were cracks in the surface.

When a sibling got in trouble, I'd sometimes catch a faint smile on his face. If I stubbed my toe or one of the kids scraped a knee, he'd show no concern, just blank indifference, or worse, a flicker of amusement. A few times, he actually jumped up and down laughing, like someone else's pain was a joke.

I didn't understand what I was seeing. I thought maybe he just hadn't learned how to respond to emotion, like so many traumatized kids, he was still figuring out how to live in a normal family. But it was more than that. When other people were in pain was the only time I saw any real emotion from him. I didn't recognize it for what it was: an early sign of something dangerous brewing beneath the surface.

Manny came to me at six years old, and I came to him full of hope. I was young, idealistic, and full of faith. I truly believed that if I loved him enough, if I taught him about Jesus, wrapped him in safety, and poured my whole heart into him, then his wounds would eventually heal. I thought he'd come to see me as his mom, and we'd build a happy, healthy life together.

* * *

But that's not what happened. Not even close. Instead of healing, we unraveled, quietly and painfully, torn apart by wounds too deep for love alone to mend.

Lessons in the Wilderness

The years with Manny were my wilderness.

Not the kind you hike through for a weekend and return refreshed, but the kind where you don't know if you'll make it out, and the landmarks are pain, exhaustion, and unanswered questions.

In Scripture, the wilderness was never wasted. God led His people there to teach them dependence, to strip away false security, and to show them that He alone could provide what they truly needed. In my wilderness, I learned the same.

I learned that my strength was never enough, but His never ran out.

I learned that love is not proven in the ease of a relationship but in the choice to keep showing up when it costs everything.

I learned that God's presence is not diminished by chaos; sometimes it is most visible there.

Looking back, I see that I was never alone, not on the longest nights, not in the moments I felt like a failure, not even when my prayers seemed to bounce off the ceiling. He was there, sustaining me one breath at a time.

If you are in your own wilderness, whether in adoption, parenting, or another battle entirely, take heart. The God who brought His people out of Egypt, who led them through the desert with a pillar of cloud by day and fire by night, still leads His children today. And when the wilderness ends, you will see that His faithfulness was never in question.

"The Lord will fight for you; you need only to be still." – Exodus 14:14

* * *

Prayer:

       God, the wilderness feels endless and my heart is heavy. Some days I'm exhausted just trying to breathe. But You, Lord, are the steady breath beneath my chaos, the unseen strength when mine fails. Help me hold on when I can't see the way. Teach me to surrender control and find peace in Your presence, even when answers don't come. Remind me that this wilderness is shaping me, refining me, and that Your faithfulness is the quiet anchor I cling to. Carry me through the night, and lead me into the dawn. Amen.

3

From the moment Gio came into our home, I knew there was something different about him. His eyes carried the weight of a past he couldn't put into words, but beneath the layers of pain, there was a tenderness and a spark of goodness that trauma hadn't fully smothered.

Gio wasn't easy. He came with wounds that bled into our daily lives. Rage, confusion, fear: it all cycled through him unpredictably. But even at his worst, there were glimmers. A kindness he couldn't completely hide. A smile that surfaced when he felt safe, even if just for a moment.

Gio's story isn't one of perfect transformation. It's the story of a boy who wanted to be good, even when the pain pulled him the other way. A story of falling and getting up, of pushing people away while longing to be held close.

There were seasons of chaos with Gio, deep and aching chaos, but there were also moments of light that made us believe healing was possible. His life taught me that redemption is messy and hard-fought, but it is real. Not every wound is healed, not every behavior fixed, but there was progress. There was beauty in the becoming.

From the start, Gio was tenderhearted, even if he didn't know how to show it well. He wanted to be loved, even though he didn't always know how to receive love. There were scars inside him: wounds from neglect, confusion, fear, but also a softness that kept trying to rise to the surface.

* * *

With Gio, I always felt like there was a real chance at healing. It wouldn't come easily, but it was possible. And that made all the difference.

Gio came from the same dark beginning as Manny. Same biological mother. Same chaotic, neglectful home. But as far as we know, he was spared the worst of what Manny endured. The stories we uncovered over time, horrific truths of how their mother sold her older children to men, seem to begin when the kids turned about five.

Gio was rescued just before that line was crossed. Barely. We believe something happened to him, his eyes carried too much sorrow for a little boy, but what it was, we still don't know. There are gaps in his story, missing pieces that no file or caseworker could ever fill in.

Even though Gio may have escaped the worst that Manny endured, he was still emotionally scarred from what he endured and he walked straight into a battlefield when he entered our home. Manny targeted him almost immediately. I tried so hard to keep them apart, to protect Gio, to create some small pocket of peace just for him, but Manny had a way of fixating, especially on Gio. And that fixation was never kind.

For years, I lived in a state of hyper-vigilance, doing my best to outsmart Manny, to guard Gio's spirit from further breaking. It's one thing to adopt a child from trauma; it's another entirely to bring them into a home where trauma is still active, still lurking down the hallway. And yet, somehow, Gio kept holding on to his sweetness. Even when life, Manny, tried to tear it from him.

Gio came to us when he was four, almost five.

I still remember the phone call. The caseworker's voice was chipper in that practiced, paper-thin way social workers sometimes have when they've said the same speech a hundred times to a hundred families. I was standing in the kitchen folding towels, the hum of the dishwasher behind me, when the phone rang.

"There's a sibling set we're trying to place," she said. "Two boys. The younger one is four. Well, almost five. His birthday's in a couple of weeks."

There was a pause, like she was debating whether to say more. Then, she added, "Another family was about to take him, but they just backed out."

I didn't ask at first. I thought maybe something scary had come up; maybe a behavior issue, a medical diagnosis. But her voice gave it away: not tense or apologetic, just tired. So I asked. "Why'd they back out?"

She sighed softly. "They said they don't... 'do birthdays.'"

I stood there, towel half-folded in my hands, blinking. "I'm sorry. What?"

"Yeah," she said, trying to soften it. "They didn't want to 'start something' or 'set a precedent for the other foster kids in the home.' It's... pretty clear they were in it for the money. Not that there's much. But still, they didn't want to spend any of it on a party or a gift. Said it wasn't worth it."

She didn't say more, but she didn't have to. The unspoken truth hung there between us. They weren't in this to love kids. They were in it to collect checks. And a birthday, this boy's birthday, was just an expense they didn't want.

I felt my stomach twist. Not out of shock, but out of sorrow. That a child could be dismissed over something as simple and sacred as a birthday. That the world could shrink his worth down to a budget line item.

"We do birthdays," I said.

There was a pause, and then a smile in her voice. "I thought you might."

And just like that, their no became our yes.

I didn't know much about the boys at that point. Most of the call was about Gio. She said he was quiet. Observant. Sweet. Maybe shy. She didn't use the word "traumatized," they rarely did, but she mentioned that he was "used to being overlooked." That phrase stayed with me.

As for the older boy, Manny, he was barely mentioned. Just a sentence here or there, tucked between details about Gio. "His brother's with him," she said once. And another time, "The older one's had a harder time in care." That was it. No stories. No context. No warning.

At the time, I was so focused on the boy with the birthday no one wanted to celebrate that I missed the shadow looming ahead him. I didn't know that Manny's silence held as much weight as Gio's sweetness; that where Gio had learned to survive by shrinking in, Manny had survived by pushing back. I didn't know the storm we were walking into.

But I did know this: Gio was ours. And from the moment I said yes, from the second I pictured a birthday cake with five candles and his name on top, I wanted him there. Not for a check. Not for a label. Just because he was worth celebrating.

From the moment he arrived, it was clear he was different. Yes, he had come from the same traumatic background as Manny. Yes, he bore the same scars of neglect, malnutrition, and survival. He'd been left to hydrate with beer, suffered physical abuse, and was barely saved from being trafficked, a horror his older brother could not escape. By the time he was five, Gio had already survived a level of danger and pain most people never experience in their entire life.

But Gio still had something left in him that many trauma kids lose: tenderness. He had a sweetness that flickered through even in the worst moments. He wanted to be loved. He wanted to belong. But survival had taught him lessons we would have to carefully unteach.

I'll never forget his first weekend with us. He didn't speak much, and when he did, the words were halting and broken. Stilted. He came from a Spanish-speaking home, and we knew no Spanish. We kept fumbling through basic phrases, trying to find ways to connect. "¿Quieres comer?" "¿Agua?" I butchered the pronunciations, and he stared at me with wide, guarded eyes, trying to decode what this new world expected of him.

A new family. A new language. All within the span of a day.

We decided to do something fun: a family outing with bounce houses and other activities. At the first bounce house, he stood at the entrance for a long time, watching other kids launch themselves into the inflatable maze with squeals of delight. He was curious but hesitant. His body leaned toward fun, but his mind pulled him back toward caution. I gave him a gentle nudge. "Go on, it's okay. I'll be right here."

He climbed up slowly, gripping the inflated ladder. I let out a small breath. Progress.

But then came the moment.

The attendant, a teenage girl in a bright yellow volunteer shirt, reached out to help him down the other side. She was smiling, kind, doing her job. But to Gio, a stranger's hand reaching for his body was no small thing. It was a threat. A trigger. A shadow of something he'd survived.

In a flash, before anyone could react, his tiny fist shot out. It came fast, hard, instinctive, and landed squarely on her nose. A full-force punch from a tiny, but strong, little boy who didn't yet know he was safe.

She recoiled with a cry of pain, hands flying to her face. Her eyes wide with shock. Around us, the crowd hushed in that awful way crowds do when something socially unacceptable happens in public. A ripple of silence, then murmurs.

And me? I knew.

I knew that punch wasn't about violence. It wasn't cruelty. It was survival. That raised fist was protection, not malice. He wasn't trying to hurt her; he was trying not to be hurt again.

But that didn't mean I could excuse it. I had to kneel down, take his trembling shoulders in my hands, and tell him firmly but gently, "No hitting. That's not okay. She wasn't trying to hurt you."

* * *

I had to teach him boundaries, even when his fear blurred the lines. I had to hold the line. He was not having my correction. He tried desperately to escape my hands on his arms trying to land blow after blow. He was in a full blown rage trying to hit anyone within range.

Around us, I could feel the eyes. The other parents. The volunteers. The whispered judgment. I was That mom with Those kids.

They didn't know. How could they?

They didn't know he'd lived in a home where hands didn't help, they harmed. Where reaching out meant pain, not care. Where birthday parties were skipped, and food was earned with silence. They saw a disobedient, wild child and a clueless parent. They didn't see a scared boy trying to make sense of a world that had never been safe.

But I saw him.

I would come to know Gio deeply through the battles, the breakthroughs, the setbacks, and the miracles. His story, unlike Manny's, would teach me about redemption. And about the cost of hope.

This is why I am so slow to judge others. You never really know someone's story. For years, people judged my kids by how they behaved in public not realizing those behaviors were rooted in deep trauma, not bad parenting.

Even as they grew into teenagers, many assumed I "had them long enough," so any poor choices they made must be my fault. Other parents assumed my strict rules made me a bad mom and didn't realize they were necessary for our home filled with kids healing from trauma. Healing from trauma isn't quick. It can take years, decades, or even a lifetime to unlearn what abuse and neglect taught a child about the world.

Those misunderstanding from friends and Gio's early public outbursts of anger led to more isolation for our family. Not only were we constantly trying to protect others from Manny's dangerous behaviors, but we also had to brace ourselves for judgment when Gio, still learning how to navigate safe touch and boundaries, would react in fear sometimes hitting someone who got too close. I can't count the times I felt people's eyes on us in the grocery store, at church, at community events watching, judging, assuming.

Eventually, it was just easier to stay home. Interacting with others became more of a chore than a comfort. There's only so much explaining you can do before the exhaustion wins. But I never stopped wishing people understood: trauma doesn't disappear just because a child is adopted into a loving home.

Love helps. It helps a lot, but healing takes more than love. It takes time. Patience. Safety. And mercy from others for the child as well as for the adoptive parents.

Gio didn't heal quickly or completely. There were still hard days, still setbacks that made me wonder if we were making any progress at all. But even in the chaos, he kept reaching for connection, for safety, for love. That quiet perseverance and the steady rising after each fall is what made his story beautiful. Not perfect. But precious. And worth every moment.

Lessons in the Wilderness

Gio's story reminds me that redemption often comes wrapped in struggle. The beauty of his journey wasn't in a perfect transformation but in the small, stubborn steps toward healing. It was in the way he kept trying, even when fear pulled him backward. It was in the sweetness he refused to surrender, even when life kept trying to take it.

In the wilderness of trauma, progress can be painfully slow. It can be so easy to lose heart when the behaviors don't vanish, when the scars don't fade as quickly as you wish. But God doesn't measure growth the way we do. He sees the heart that keeps reaching toward the light, even when the shadows linger.

When I think of Gio, I think of the God who does not break a bruised reed or snuff out a smoldering wick. I think of a Father who celebrates every tiny step toward wholeness, who sees beauty in becoming, even when the becoming is messy.

If you are walking beside someone whose wounds run deep, don't despise the small beginnings. Celebrate the flickers of tenderness. Hold on to hope when progress feels invisible. God is still at work quietly, faithfully, and completely.

"A bruised reed He will not break, and a smoldering wick He will not snuff out. In faithfulness He will bring forth justice." – Isaiah 42:3

Prayer:

Father, thank You for Your tender heart that never breaks a bruised reed or snuffs out a faint flicker of hope. In the wilderness of struggle, help me to celebrate the small steps of healing and to trust Your faithful work beneath the surface. When progress feels slow and shadows linger, remind me that You see every effort, every flicker of light, and that Your grace is enough to carry us through. Strengthen my faith to keep walking forward, knowing You are making all things new. Amen.

4

Some stories don't begin with beauty. They start in the shadows and in conditions no child should ever have to survive. Judy's story is one of those. Before she became the joyful, resilient young woman we know today, she came to us from a place of silent suffering.

Her past was filled with things she couldn't say. Things she may not even remember, but her body remembered. Her behavior remembered. And slowly, we began to learn just how much she had endured.

When she arrived in our home, Judy was covered in cockroach bites from head to toe. I didn't even know cockroaches could bite like that until I saw her. But apparently, if there are enough of them, they do. I remember feeling stunned and sick as I took in the damage across her small body.

This wasn't just poverty or neglect. This was infestation, filth, and abandonment. She had been left in a crib she couldn't escape while vermin crawled across her skin, biting her as she cried, unheard and untouched.

She had been trapped there. For hours. No rescue. No comfort. That was the beginning of her story. A story that now radiates joy, but began in silent horror.

I first saw Judy in a crowded courtroom. Her two older brothers and I were waiting for our names to be called. It wasn't part of the plan to take a third child. Our household already included two biological kids, and I was pregnant, but when we learned Judy had been placed in a foster home alone, separated from her brothers simply because no family would take all three, we knew we couldn't leave her behind.

A week after that decision, I showed up at the courthouse with a satchel of snacks and a few toys to keep Gio and Manny occupied. As we waited, the social worker brought Judy in. Her tiny frame seemed to shiver under the fluorescent lights. She paused in the doorway, watching her brothers, unsure of where to go.

As she stood there, I took in her appearance. She looked like a forgotten child, scooped up at the last minute and dropped into this moment with no preparation, no care. Her clothes didn't fit: baggy and mismatched, clearly taken from a bin of donations. Her socks didn't match, and her shoes, if you could call them that, were scuffed, too big, one missing a shoelace, and the other worn clean through the sole.

And her hair... Oh, her hair. It stopped me.

She had this long, tangled layer in the back, like someone had once tried to grow it out, but the top... the top was something else entirely. Cropped into a too-short, choppy bowl shape, it looked as if someone had placed a mixing bowl on her head and cut around it with dull scissors and then gotten bored and never finished. The unevenness made her look both older and younger than she was, as if her face hadn't yet decided how much of her life to reveal.

But then she saw me, "the snack lady," as she would later call me and something shifted. Tentatively, she inched forward. I reached into my bag and offered her a cracker.

She took it. Then, without warning, she turned, backed up, and sat down right in my lap.

Just like that.

There was no eye contact. No asking permission. Just a quiet trust, fragile and inexplicable. As though some part of her had decided, This one. This woman is safe.

* * *

I didn't move at first. I was afraid even my breath might spook her.

But she didn't move either. She settled against me with the weight of a child who hadn't been held enough. She wasn't stiff, but she wasn't soft either. She was somewhere in between, her little body poised to flee at any moment, yet staying. Choosing to stay.

I reached into my bag again and pulled out more snacks. A second cracker. A small, individually wrapped granola bar. A fruit pouch. I laid them out in my palm like offerings.

Her brothers tried to take the food from her hands, reaching with the casual entitlement of boys who had learned to grab first and ask later. They were used to adults looking the other way and used to food being a competition, not a gift. But this time, the rules were different.

"No," I said gently but firmly. "This is for Judy."

They pouted, deflated by the unexpected boundary. But Judy... she beamed. Not in a loud or boastful way. It was just a quiet, glowing smile. Like someone who had never been protected before, never been prioritized.

She wasn't used to anyone standing between her and the bullies. She wasn't used to being the one who got to keep her food.

For once, no one was taking her meal.

And she savored it, not just the food, but the moment.

She didn't speak. She only reached, took the next cracker, and began to eat.

Slowly at first. Then faster. Not like she was enjoying it, but like she'd learned not to waste a moment when food was in front of her. She chewed with her lips pressed together, crumbs dusting her shirt, eyes still wide open. She kept glancing at the bag, as if wondering if there would be more, or if this kindness was temporary.

I whispered gently, "It's okay. There's more."

* * *

She didn't answer. But she leaned in a little closer.

There we sat: me on a cold vinyl chair in a fluorescent-lit court room lobby, and this tiny girl with a terrible haircut and mismatched shoes, curled in my lap like she'd always been there. The social worker kept talking somewhere behind us, explaining policies and visitation and medical forms, but none of it mattered in that moment. All I could focus on was the weight of her. The way she rested her head against my chest.

In that moment, I felt her whole story press into me: the hungry, cautious hope for comfort.

Then the social worker called her name.

"Judy? Let's go!."

The words were professional, lacking love. She was ready to be done working for the day. Judy's small body stiffened in my lap. Her chewing stopped mid-bite. I felt her go tense, like a startled animal sensing danger. She turned toward the voice, then back to me, panic blooming in her eyes.

She didn't speak right away. It was like her brain had to catch up to what was being asked of her.

Time to leave.

Again.

Her short, choppy hair bounced as she twisted around, searching the room like it had betrayed her. She looked at the bag of snacks still sitting beside us. She looked at the brothers who, for once, hadn't taken what was hers and then back at me, "the snack lady." Her face crumpled.

"No!" she screamed, the word bursting out of her like it had been waiting just beneath the surface. One moment, she was calm, content even, snuggled in my lap with crumbs on her shirt and a cracker in hand. The next, it was as if someone had flipped a switch. Her joy shattered in an instant, replaced by raw, panicked fury..

Something inside her broke loose, and it came out like a wave.

"No!" she screamed again, her voice sharp and broken.

Before I could react, she jerked away from me, thrashing as she slid from my lap. Her tiny hands pushed off my knees, her legs kicking wildly as she tumbled to the floor like a doll thrown from a shelf. She landed hard on her side, then flipped onto her back, fists pounding the linoleum with frantic, aimless fury. Her tiny fists pounded the carpet, her voice hoarse and cracking from her shrill screams.

She didn't have the words to name what was happening, but her body knew.

She had tasted safety, and now it was being pulled away.

The social worker stepped forward, clearly impatient, her smile tight and forced. "It's just the transition. She'll calm down in the car." There was no softness in her tone. There was just a hint of irritation, as if Judy's meltdown was an inconvenience, a box to check, a routine disruption in an already long day. She didn't kneel. Didn't reach out. Just waited, arms crossed, keys dangling impatiently from one hand.

But I knew it wasn't just the transition. It was grief.

Even at two and a half, Judy knew enough to recognize when love was slipping through her fingers. She had only just learned our names, or invented names for us in her toddler way, and now she was being told to let go. Again. To trust another stranger. Again. To leave her brothers and go somewhere all alone, again.

I knelt beside her, rubbing her back. She didn't want comfort. She wanted permanence. She wanted to stay.

Her cries softened into gasping hiccups, but she didn't look at me. She just repeated it, over and over, like a plea she hoped someone might grant if she said it enough times.

* * *

"Snack lady… brothers… don't go…"

My heart broke wide open. She was terrified, torn between the comfort of my lap and the unknown place she was being sent to, alone once more. I knelt beside her, stroking her hair and whispering that her brothers were just outside, that soon we'd all be together. But her body trembled with panic until the social worker finally took her hand and dragged her away. I can still see her small frame being pulled through the door, her cries echoing behind her.

A week later, it finally happened: she walked through our front door. Her eyes were wide, her face lit with nerves and flickers of hope. She ran to me and asked for more snacks. Gone was the courtroom fear. In its place, a surge of relief filled the room.

"Snack lady," she said, expectantly holding out a dirty little hand.

I didn't have any snacks right then. She paused, turning to her brothers, eyes flicking between them and me. None of us knew what came next. I wasn't fully "Mom" to her yet, but in that moment, I ached to be.

That's when it hit me: our family had grown from two to five with another on the way in the span of two weeks. And even one more child was worth every unknown, every sleepless night, every rearranged plan. With Judy there vulnerable, trusting, still learning what safety felt like, everything we'd risked found its anchor. In her uncertain gaze, I saw our future. A promise that no matter how tangled the road, she would never walk it alone.

We don't know much about her early life for certain. But her behavior told us what words couldn't. Like her brothers, she hoarded food. It was instinctive, almost primal. She'd hide it under beds, behind furniture, in shoes and pockets. If I turned my back, she'd dart into the pantry and grab fistfuls of anything she could find, shoving it into her mouth so fast she would choke.

At daycare, she came home with constant incident reports:

* * *

"Judy choked during snack time."

"Judy had to be helped after stuffing food into her mouth."

The daycare workers didn't understand. "We go over snack rules every day," one of them told me, exasperated. "Take small bites. Wait your turn. Use your spoon. But she just… doesn't listen."

I wanted to explain that this wasn't defiance. It was survival.

Once, I got a call in the middle of the day. Judy had choked again. She had choked badly this time. A teacher had to wrap her arms around Judy's little torso and heave until the chunk of food dislodged. She was shaken but unharmed. "She went back to playing right after," the teacher said, sounding surprised. "Didn't cry. Didn't say a word."

Of course she didn't. She'd already learned not to make a fuss. She had learned to move on quickly, to keep smiling, to pretend like nothing hurt.

We often imagine trauma as loud, violent, or explosive. But with Judy, it whispered. It hid in granola bars stuffed in shoes. In the way she froze at the sight of bugs. In the way she clung to food like it was life itself. She never told us what happened in those early years. She didn't have to. Her body spoke for her.

And yet, even then, there was something in her that wanted to hope.

She didn't arrive hardened or angry like her brothers. She came wounded. Yes, deeply, but she already yearned for connection. She was full of fear, but not full of hate. She wanted to belong. She wanted to be safe.

We often speak of trauma as something to outrun. But for Judy, healing looked more like learning to breathe again. In those first weeks, I noticed how her breath would catch whenever someone came too close. Over time, she let us hold her without tensing. She let us sing lullabies without flinching. She let us feed her applesauce which was soft, sweet, and sustaining without choking on panic. Each small moment was a step away from the darkness.

* * *

This is where Judy's story begins: not in light, not with smiles or laughter or safety. It begins in a crib full of cockroaches, in a body covered with bites, in a toddler's frantic fear of hunger. But that's only the beginning.

This is the first chapter in a redemption story so miraculous, so breathtaking, that even now I can hardly believe it. Judy didn't just survive. She didn't just heal.

She became something radiant.

But first, she had to be rescued from the dark.

Lessons in the Wilderness

Judy's journey teaches us that God often meets us not in the moments of strength, but in the depths of our brokenness. When wounds are too deep for words and healing feels slow, it is the Savior's gentle presence that carries us through the darkness.

The wilderness of trauma and fear is a sacred place where God's grace shines brightest. It is there that He comforts the hurting, restores the weary, and begins the work of redemption in even the smallest, most tender moments. Healing may look like fragile trust, hesitant breaths, and quiet steps toward hope, but these are the footprints of His love drawing us closer to wholeness.

If you find yourself walking through a wilderness of pain, remember: Christ is near. He is the Good Shepherd who seeks the lost, binds up the brokenhearted, and offers rest to the weary soul. His grace is not dependent on our perfection or readiness; it flows freely into the cracks of our lives, bringing light where shadows once reigned.

Take heart in the promise that God is not distant in your suffering but is close, drawing you out of darkness and into the radiant hope of new life in Him.

"The LORD is close to the brokenhearted and saves those who are crushed in

spirit." — *Psalm 34:18*

Prayer:

Lord Jesus, You are near to the brokenhearted and close to those crushed in spirit. When my wounds feel too deep and healing seems slow, meet me in my wilderness. Carry me gently with Your grace and fill the darkest places with Your light. Help me to trust Your steady presence and to find rest in Your loving care. Thank You for being my Good Shepherd, always seeking, always healing, always restoring. Amen.

5

There's a saying: stand on a chair and try to pull someone up. It's far easier for them to pull you down. That's what it was like adopting Manny.

Never in my wildest imagination did I think a child could disrupt an entire family system, but he did. For about a year, he hid his mental illness well in what we call the "honeymoon phase." I genuinely believed we were making progress. I thought he was healing.

If you're hearing me talk about Manny and thinking I sound like a cynical or cold mother, I understand. I might have thought the same thing once. Before I lived it.

Until you've lived it, you can't truly understand what it's like to raise a child who is terrifying. A child who might, in clinical terms, be a literal psychopath. Not every child can be saved from their trauma. Some wounds go so deep they can't be undone. That was Manny.

I had other children in the home besides Manny, and as the honeymoon phase faded, I found myself more and more in the role of protector: shielding them from him. My life became the chair analogy all over again. I was the mother on the chair, reaching down to lift Manny up. But instead of rising, he pulled me, and our entire family, down with him.

My other children were slipping under his shadow. I was protecting and shielding them from him, but in doing so, I was unraveling, losing pieces of myself in the daily battle of trying to parent a child who simply could not be parented.

I used to be the kind of mom who never raised her voice. I was patient, calm, steady. Until Manny.

Little by little, I began losing my cool: yelling, snapping, unraveling in ways I never had before. I wasn't equipped to deal with the kind of extreme behaviors he brought into our home. What was once a place of peace and safety became filled with chaos and dysfunction and it was all centered around Manny.

We thought we were being obedient to Christ, saying yes to a child who needed love and a family. But that obedience was tearing our family apart.

It started subtly as the honeymoon period came to an end in that first year. Small things at first like odd behaviors and uneasy feelings. By the time he turned seven, the lying and sneaking began in earnest. We knew we couldn't trust him. What we didn't yet understand was that trust was only the beginning of what we were about to lose.

Manny shared a room with his brothers, but then we discovered the unthinkable that he was attempting to act out on them the very same abusive behaviors he had been rescued from. It was a moment that shattered my hope not just for his healing, but for our safety. I realized in that instant that love alone could not undo what had been done to him.

We did everything we could to keep everyone safe. We went to social workers, desperate for help. But they told us there was nothing they could do. Because Manny was adopted, he was legally ours. If we tried to give him back, they warned us we'd be charged with child abandonment. They would take all our children, and we would likely go to jail.

They also said that since he was now "ours," there was no financial assistance for residential treatment. If we wanted help, we'd have to pay out of pocket tens of thousands of dollars a year we simply didn't have.

* * *

At the time, we were poor. We had enough to eat and live, but not enough to pay for long-term residential care.

With no help coming, we had to become our own safety net. We put bells on the beds so we'd hear if anyone got up at night. Doors stayed open at all times. Manny was never allowed to be alone with another child. Ever. Many nights were spent with me on the floor of their room.

Many adults didn't understand the extreme precautions we had in place for Manny. To them, we looked overly strict. Controlling, even. And they weren't afraid to say so.

I remember one of my husband's close family members pulling him aside and criticizing us, saying it was cruel that we had different rules for Manny than for the other kids. No effort to understand. No questions. Just judgment. Judgment from people who had no idea what we were living with behind closed doors.

Eventually, we had to stop leaving the kids with that family member. She refused to believe how serious the situation was and wouldn't follow the safety measures we needed to protect everyone. It simply wasn't safe.

You might wonder: Why didn't she believe us? If Manny was so dangerous, wouldn't it be obvious?

Manny was a master manipulator. I often said I was grateful to God his IQ was on the lower side because if he had paired his manipulation with high intelligence, we would have been in even more serious trouble. He could fool anyone. He could put on the mask of the perfect child for months at a time.

His true self only came out slowly and only around me, the one who was with him all day, every day. Even in the evenings, when his father got home, the mask would slip back on. He knew how to charm, how to disarm, and how to hide.

When my husband came home from work, I'd unload the day telling him all the horrible things Manny had done. He listened. He believed me. But it put him in an impossible position: trying to support me fully while watching Manny play the part of the sweet, devoted son the moment he walked in the door.

I never imagined a young child could manipulate so effectively, but Manny did.

At one playdate, the host's friend was visiting. She must've been in her late sixties, with soft curls and a voice that had probably once read bedtime stories to perfect children. At one point, I stepped into the hallway to help another child zip up their coat, and when I returned, I saw this woman whom I had only met hours earlier crouched beside Manny, one hand resting on his shoulder.

She was whispering. I couldn't hear the words, but I could see his face a smirk of satisfaction. I knew the smile he made when he felt like he won. I wondered what he had won, but then her voice rose just enough to catch it:

"I'm so sorry your mean mom won't let you play with the other kids."

She said it with a small laugh, like it was a joke. But it wasn't. Not to him. And certainly not to me.

I froze in the doorway, coat half-zipped in my hands.

"Mean mom."

That's what she saw when she looked at me.

Not a mother protecting the other children. Not a mother balancing risk and responsibility with the weight of every decision. Just a woman being too strict. Too uptight. Too unwilling to "let a kid be a kid."

She didn't see the real reason.

She didn't see how Manny could turn in a second. How his charm could melt into rage with barely a breath between. This stranger to me only saw a sad little boy not allowed to go play. I saw a potential disaster waiting at the bottom of those basement stairs.

* * *

I kept my mouth shut, but inside, my thoughts were screaming.

If I let him go down there, your kids could end up hurt in the same ways he was hurt by his birth mother.

Is that really better? Just so he's not left out? So you feel better about what it looks like, even if it's not safe for anyone?

Would you still think I was "mean" if he left bruises on your son? Would you be so quick to whisper sympathy into his ear if you had to pull your daughter away sobbing because Manny got her alone when no one was looking?

That's the thing about trauma. It hides well. Until it doesn't.

So yes, I stood there and said nothing. I let her think what she wanted to think. Let Manny feel misunderstood, again. Let myself carry the judgment, the eye rolls, the whispered pity.

Because that's what trauma parenting sometimes requires, being the villain in someone else's story, so you don't let a much worse story unfold downstairs, out of sight.

But moments like that only fed Manny's growing instability. He discovered that all he had to do was act sweet and innocent, and adults would line up to believe him. I became the villain in his performance: the strict, unloving mother in contrast to the charming child. And he relished it. It was a game to him. One he was getting better at. One he was winning.

As these kinds of interactions with others became more frequent, we began to withdraw from the world. I had very few friends, and we took even fewer outings as a family especially when Manny was with us. Eventually, we only left the house when he was in school, because the backlash from those who didn't understand what we were living with was just too much. What we desperately needed was support and wise counsel. What we got instead was judgment.

Early on, we tried hiring sitters so my husband and I could catch a breath, just a short break from the storm. We always gave sitters clear, strict instructions. But again, no one ever believed things were really that bad. Manny could charm anyone. He had me fooled for a year before I saw his true colors. In hindsight I should have realized that how could a babysitter, there for only two hours, see through the performance?

Looking back, I think that was the most dangerous part, not the rage, but the mask.

When sitters began reporting back what they described as "playful curiosity" from Manny, but what I recognized instantly as predatory behavior, we knew we had to stop using sitters altogether. No one, it seemed, could keep the children in our home safe from Manny except my husband and me. With us there, the other children were safe. Manny couldn't hurt them. With anyone else in charge, that was not the case.

That was the final wall closing in. We were cut off. Completely. No friends, because they judged us for the strict rules that kept Manny from participating. No date nights, because we couldn't trust anyone to protect our other children in our absence. Not even family help because they refused to follow the safeguards we had in place.

I was completely alone.

The kind of alone that comes not from solitude, but from being disbelieved and unseen. I was carrying the full weight of Manny's needs, his danger, and the fear of what could happen if I ever let my guard down, even for a moment.

It began to eat away at me. I started to feel like a prisoner in my own home, always on high alert. I didn't sleep well, constantly listening for bells on beds, footsteps in the hallway, anything that might signal danger. My body was exhausted, but my mind couldn't rest.

Spiritually, I wrestled with guilt and confusion. I had stepped out in obedience and opened our home in faith and now it felt like that obedience was slowly crushing us. I kept crying out to God, asking why. Why give us this child if love wasn't going to be enough? Why call us to something that seemed to be tearing our family apart?

And still, no answers came. Just more days of silence, fear, and exhaustion.

I began to lose pieces of myself: my joy, my confidence, my laughter. I felt like a shell of the mom I used to be. The peace that once filled our home was gone, and in its place was survival mode. There wasn't room for anything else.

There's a kind of emotional distress that comes from being responsible for preventing trauma. From having to see danger where others see a child. From being told you're overreacting, when deep down you know that your vigilance might be the only thing standing between safety and disaster.

And in the middle of all that, I still had to smile for the other kids. I still had to pack lunches, oversee schoolwork, read bedtime stories. I had to keep showing up as the mom they needed while carrying the kind of emotional burden most people couldn't begin to imagine.

In raising Manny, I lost myself. People now tell me that I handled the difficulties of adoption so well. No, I didn't. I became depressed, lost my spark, bled in silence, shattered in private. I wore a smile that lied better than any mask could.

I wasn't becoming someone cruel or cold; I was becoming someone frayed and fragile from the weight of it all. My tenderness hadn't left me; it was buried beneath exhaustion and fear. I missed the version of myself who felt calm, light-hearted, safe in her own home.

And it took a toll, not just on me, but on our marriage too. My husband was doing what he could, working long hours to provide for us, and then coming home to chaos and crisis. But while he was away at work, I bore the brunt of the protection. I was the one listening for footsteps, managing meltdowns, guarding the other children. It created a quiet divide between us; one made not of blame, but of sheer imbalance. He didn't fully see the battle I was fighting all day long, and I didn't know how to explain the constant fear I lived in.

* * *

We were both trying our best. But our best, in those days, never felt like enough.

I had believed love would be enough. But sometimes, love alone isn't what saves a child. Sometimes, it's not even enough to survive them.

Lessons in the Wilderness

There are seasons in parenting, and in life, when love, though powerful, is simply not enough. Sometimes, we walk through wildernesses so dark and tangled that all we can do is cling to God's promises and lean into His strength.

Manny's story is a heartbreaking reminder that some wounds run deep, and some battles are beyond what human love alone can heal. In those moments of exhaustion, fear, and sorrow, we face a profound truth: God's grace is sufficient even when our own strength fails.

The wilderness can feel isolating. It can strip away joy and hope. But it is also a place where God meets us in our weakness, offering rest to the weary and courage to the faint-hearted. He never promises that the journey will be easy or that pain will disappear quickly, but He does promise His presence will never leave us.

When love feels insufficient, God's love remains. His peace transcends understanding. And His power works in the broken places where healing seems impossible.

If you find yourself in a season where love isn't enough, hold fast to this: You are not alone. The One who carried the cross for you carries your burdens too. He is with you in the shadows, holding you up when the chair feels shaky and the weight unbearable.

"My grace is sufficient for you, for my power is made perfect in weakness." — *2 Corinthians 12:9*

Prayer:

God, in the moments when my love feels too small and my strength is gone, remind me that Your grace is enough. Carry me through the dark wilderness when I feel alone and weary. Help me to lean fully on You, trusting that Your power is made perfect in my weakness. May Your peace fill the broken places and Your presence be my refuge and strength. Thank You for never leaving me, even when the road is hard. In Jesus' name, Amen.

6

I still remember Gio's first doctor's appointment with us. What should have been a routine check-up revealed more than words ever could. As the nurse gently examined him, it was clear something in his past had left invisible scars. The moment they had to touch him, his body tensed with fear, and he began to cry and thrash.

It wasn't the kind of fuss kids make when they're scared of shots; this was deep, protective terror. By the end of the visit, the nurse quietly slipped out of the room in tears herself. Not because he had hurt her, he hadn't, but because his trauma was written all over his little body, and it was impossible not to feel it as she examined him.

Gio was very different from Manny in how he carried his pain. Where Manny often turned outward with his anger, Gio turned inward. If someone got too close and he couldn't protect himself by lashing out, he would harm himself instead.

At just five years old, he would punch or scratch his own arms, sometimes until he bled. It was his way of coping and trying to reclaim control in a world that had taken so much from him.

It could happen over something as simple as me saying, "No."

Not harshly. Not with anger. Just a gentle correction. A redirect. "Let's try that again." "Make a better choice." "Please don't throw the toy." Any of those could be the spark.

* * *

And like a switch flipping, everything would change.

One minute, Gio would be standing there fidgety but fine, eyes tracking the room, maybe annoyed or restless like any kid his age. And the next... it was like the floor gave way beneath him.

His whole face would crumble. His shoulders would fold inward like he was trying to disappear. And then the war would begin.

But it wasn't against me. Not really.

It was against himself.

He'd start hitting himself. Small strikes at first, quick slaps to the side of his head. Then harder. A fist to the temple. Scratching at his arms, his face. Screaming, but not at me. Screaming at something I couldn't see. Something I couldn't reach. His own shame. His own terror. His own wiring that told him if you mess up, you must be punished. And if no one punishes you, do it yourself.

I remember one day in particular. He'd knocked over a block tower his sibling was building on purpose, with that flicker of mischief in his eye. Just regular kid stuff. I stepped in calmly.

"Gio, that wasn't kind. Please help rebuild it."

That was all I said.

And it shattered him.

"No! No! NO!" he cried, backing into the wall like I'd raised my hand though I hadn't moved an inch. Then his fists went to his head, pounding. His whole body convulsed as he collapsed to the floor, kicking, sobbing, slapping his own face over and over like he was trying to erase himself.

I dropped beside him, hands out but not touching. "Gio. Stop. You're safe. I'm not mad. You're okay."

But he wasn't okay. He was lost in a storm that didn't belong in this room but had followed him here from somewhere else entirely. Somewhere darker.

And I couldn't pull him out of it.

There's a particular kind of helplessness that comes with watching your young child hurt themselves, especially when you're the trigger. When your voice, your boundary, your love is what sends them over the edge. It's like parenting a live wire. You try to guide. To discipline gently. To redirect and build trust. But sometimes, even safety looks like danger to a child who's never truly known it.

Gio punished himself not to manipulate, but to survive.

All of our kids were in therapy, and early on, the therapist began noticing patterns. She saw emerging traits in Manny that concerned her: early indicators that might align with psychopathy in older individuals. In Gio, she saw possible signs of early-onset bipolar disorder. But they were both too young for official diagnoses.

What concerned her most about Gio was how his behavior shifted once he started ADHD medication. He had been diagnosed with ADHD, and like many parents, we hoped medication would help him focus and thrive.

But what happened instead was terrifying.

It started one day after the first dose. I remember the morning clearly and how ordinary it was. The sun streaming through the windows. The smell of waffles in the toaster. Gio padding into the kitchen in his too-big Batman pajama pants. He was quiet, but that wasn't unusual.

Then he stopped.

Frozen in the middle of the hallway.

He looked down at his feet.

And screamed.

* * *

Not a frustrated yell. Not a tantrum. A scream: raw, primal, bone-deep.

He kicked off one sock violently, then the other. "Get them off! Get them off!" he shrieked, hopping from foot to foot, slapping at his legs.

"Gio, what's wrong?" I ran to him, heart already pounding.

"They're on me!" he cried. "The rats! They're in my socks. They're crawling on me! Get them OFF!"

I dropped to my knees and grabbed his legs, gently but firmly. "Gio, there's nothing there. Look. See? Nothing. Just your socks. You're okay, sweetheart."

But to him, it was real.

He flailed, trying to shake off the invisible creatures. His eyes were wide with terror, darting from the floor to the walls like he was tracking something I couldn't see. Sweat beaded at his temples. His chest rose and fell in panicked gasps.

He wasn't there with me. He was trapped somewhere else entirely.

I called my husband, and together we tried to calm him by talking low, holding him close, reassuring him that he was safe. But he kept swatting at his legs, whimpering, "They're still there… I can feel them."

I didn't know what to do. I didn't know how to bring him back.

Eventually, the episode passed. He collapsed into my lap, exhausted and confused, his little body trembling with leftover fear.

We called the psychiatrist. The medication was stopped immediately.

Thankfully, that kind of episode never happened again. The therapist told us that sometimes, ADHD medication can trigger reactions like this in children who may have underlying bipolar tendencies. It wasn't a diagnosis, just one more box to watch as he grew.

* * *

Even with all of that, Gio's heart shined. He was full of affection and had an instinctive protectiveness, especially for the younger kids in the home. It was like something deep in him had made a decision that whatever he had endured, he wouldn't let other children suffer in the same way.

I used to say, even when he was very little, that I could see him becoming a police officer someday. There was something fierce and loyal in him, something that wanted to keep others safe.

Two weeks after Gio came to live with us, he had his very first birthday party. He had never had one before. It was simple. It was just a trip to McDonald's, where we told him he could order whatever he wanted. We brought a cake, a few presents, and the kids played on the playground. But his eyes lit up like we'd taken him to Disney World.

That small moment watching him feel celebrated and special, maybe for the first time in his life stays with me even now. His story began in pain, but it was always reaching for joy.

The cake was small, but it was his. Bright blue frosting. Five flickering candles. A crown of rainbow sprinkles that stuck to our fingers when we lit the candles and pulled the matches away.

He sat at the head of the table, tiny legs dangling from the chair, a party hat crooked on his head. His eyes moved slowly, taking it all in: the balloons, the paper plates, the crayon-colored banner strung across the wall that said Happy Birthday, Gio!

Then we started to sing.

At first, he stared at us, frozen. His back stiffened slightly, like maybe he thought he was in trouble and didn't understand the rules of this strange ritual. But as the song grew louder and more confident, siblings off-key, adults trying to harmonize, his expression began to change.

His eyes went wide. His mouth opened just slightly, not to speak, but like he'd forgotten how to close it.

* * *

And then… the tears came.

Not sobs. Not sorrow. Just silent, steady tears slipping down his cheeks, carving little paths through the frosting smudge on his face.

He wasn't sad.

He was overwhelmed.

No one had ever sung to him before. Not like this. Not all together, just for him. Not with cake and candles and a table full of people clapping their hands and calling his name like he mattered.

He was five years old, and it was the first time he had been celebrated simply for existing.

When we finished the song and told him to make a wish, he just sat there, beaming through the tears, too full of joy to move.

"Do you want to blow out your candles?" I whispered.

He nodded, wiped his nose with his sleeve, then leaned forward and blew with all his might like he was trying to make up for all the birthdays he never had.

And in that moment, I realized: joy, when you're not used to it, doesn't always look like laughter.

Sometimes it looks like a stunned little boy, crying in front of a cake, because someone finally told him he was worth celebrating.

As we sang "Happy Birthday," our little five-year-old cried. Not out of sadness, but because he was overwhelmed with joy. No one had ever sung him "Happy Birthday" before. He sat there, wide-eyed, face glowing, so full of happiness he didn't know what to do with it.

That's how life with Gio has always been. There were many low moments, when his emotions ran deep and he had no way to regulate them. But alongside those dark valleys, there were mountaintop moments of genuine joy. He had a grateful heart. He knew what it was to have nothing, and so every "first" carried weight. He didn't take anything for granted.

Imagine getting to witness a child's firsts not as a baby, but as a much older child. It's a bittersweet privilege. Sweet, because they're old enough to understand and feel the full depth of what they've been given. You get to see their wonder, their gratitude. But bitter, too because those firsts should have come years earlier. There's always a quiet shadow behind their smile, a trace of sorrow for what was stolen from them.

Still, Gio's ability to feel joy, even after all the pain, was one of the most beautiful parts of his story. He taught us what it means to be thankful, to celebrate even the small things, and to find light in the cracks of a broken beginning.

Gio didn't yet know the name of the One who was healing him, but I could see God's hand all over his story taking what was broken, and slowly, gently, making something strong, tender, and full of purpose.

Lessons in the Wilderness

The journey with Gio has often felt like wandering through a wilderness: a place of uncertainty, struggle, and waiting. The wilderness is not a place we choose to be, but sometimes it is where God leads us to teach us, refine us, and draw us closer to Him.

In the wilderness, God meets us not with immediate answers, but with His presence. He walks beside us through the fear, the pain, and the confusion. He does not promise that the journey will be easy, but He promises that we will never walk it alone.

Gio's story is a powerful reminder that healing is not always quick or straightforward. Like the Israelites wandering the desert for forty years, sometimes the road to restoration is long and marked by challenges. Yet, it is in these seasons that God's refining work is often the deepest. He is shaping hearts, building endurance, and teaching trust.

* * *

When we feel overwhelmed, when our faith feels fragile, and when joy seems distant, God's grace sustains us. He reminds us that even in the wilderness, there is purpose, and even in the pain, there is hope.

As we care for those who carry deep wounds, we learn to lean not on our own understanding but on God's steadfast love and mercy. He is the Good Shepherd who seeks the lost, binds up the brokenhearted, and carries us when we cannot walk alone.

May we remember that the wilderness is not the end of the story. It is a holy place of transformation, where God's light breaks through the darkness and His promises bring new life.

"When you pass through the waters, I will be with you;
and through the rivers, they shall not overwhelm you;
when you walk through fire you shall not be burned,
and the flame shall not consume you."
— Isaiah 43:2 (ESV)

Prayer:
Lord, thank You that You walk with us through every wilderness season, never leaving us alone in our struggles or pain. Help us to trust Your presence even when healing is slow and the path is unclear. Strengthen our faith when we feel weak, and remind us that Your love and grace are always enough to carry us through. May we lean fully on You, the Good Shepherd, who binds up the brokenhearted and leads us into new life. In Jesus' name, Amen.

7

Before there was joy, there was fear. Before the healing, there was damage too deep for a two-year-old to name. And before she could smile without flinching, she had to be held tightly, day after day, through the tremors of a past her little body never asked for. This is not the whole of Judy's story, but it is where it begins.

Judy's story begins in darkness, but it ends in light. She came to us at just two and a half years old. She was young enough, we hoped, to be spared the worst of what her siblings lived through. But it didn't take long to realize that even at that tender age, her world had already left deep wounds.

Trauma doesn't wait for memory to form. Being little didn't protect her from the impact of neglect, fear, and instability.

Though the full truth of her early life is still cloudy, we believe Judy narrowly escaped being trafficked. Her mother was a prostitute. Some of her half-siblings, heartbreakingly, were sold. Judy was not spared the damage that kind of world brings to a child's soul, but by the grace of God, she was spared from the same fate.

She shared a crib in the room where her mother sold herself, and from that crib, she bore witness to the abuse of her older half siblings even though she herself was spared.

She had an intense fear of bathrooms that we never fully understood. When she came to us, she was still in diapers and had not yet begun potty training. But one day, she saw me working with her brother Gio, and something inside her shifted.

As if determined to reclaim something for herself, she made up her mind. She was done with diapers. From that moment on, she refused to wear one again. Incredibly, she potty trained herself in a single day, with no prompting or help from me. It was as if she was escaping whatever diapers had come to mean to her and taking back control, choosing the freedom of not depending on anyone to change her.

At home, she was fine.

She'd walk down the hallway in her little socks, the bathroom door left slightly ajar as she did her business like any other toddler. It was unremarkable. Routine. Safe.

But anywhere else, even the clean, cheerful restrooms at church or a friend's house, was a different story.

The moment we crossed the threshold of a new bathroom, something inside her would shatter.

Her small body would tense in my arms. Her eyes would scan every corner like she was bracing for something unseen. And then, almost without warning, she'd erupt thrashing, kicking, shrieking like the walls themselves were closing in.

It wasn't a tantrum. It wasn't testing limits.

It was terror.

One afternoon, we were visiting my sister's house which was a familiar place, filled with cousins and warmth and the smell of coffee brewing in the kitchen. Judy had been doing well, even giggling over a puzzle just ten minutes earlier. But then she whispered that she had to go potty, and I gently walked her toward the hall bathroom.

The moment she saw the toilet, she froze.

I followed her gaze and saw it. Blue water.

* * *

Just the cleaning solution. Nothing harmful. Nothing dangerous.

But to Judy, it was as if the bowl was filled with fire.

She backed away, eyes wide, fists clenched at her sides. "No! No! No!" she cried, her voice rising into a panicked wail. Then the sobs came, raw and choking, and she sank to the floor in the hallway, inconsolable.

She would rather wet herself than go near that toilet.

And honestly, sometimes she did.

There was no logic to it, at least, none that we could see. She couldn't explain the fear. Couldn't tell us what her body remembered. But it was in her eyes. In her muscles. In the way she'd shake and cry and plead with us not to make her go in there.

Whatever had happened in a bathroom before she came to us, it had written itself into her nervous system.

And we could only guess.

Had someone hurt her in a place like this? Locked her in? Used the toilet as a weapon of shame or punishment? I remember kneeling on that cold tile floor, watching her tremble and scream, and wondering what memory could make a child afraid of a toilet.

Eventually, we found a way.

It wasn't a tender breakthrough. It was desperation.

She was refusing to go. Again. Arms crossed, face tight, her whole body locked down in silent panic. I knew that look. I knew what came next. If I didn't intervene, she would soil herself, not because she was stubborn, but because her fear was bigger than her body.

So I picked her up.

* * *

She kicked and whimpered, but I carried her down the hallway to the bathroom, holding her firmly, not unkindly, but with the kind of grip that said, I will not let you drown in this.

When we got there, she wrapped her arms around my neck like a lifeline and refused to let go.

Not even a little.

She clung to me with everything she had, legs still trembling, breath hot against my shoulder. And then, without a word, she began to shimmy down. Slowly, carefully, awkwardly, she shifted her weight while still clutching my neck, adjusting just enough to sit on the toilet… without letting go.

Her body shook, but she managed it wrapped around me like ivy on a trellis, using my strength to borrow some of her own.

I didn't move. I didn't rush her. I just knelt there, bent awkwardly, letting her cling to me while she did the hardest thing her mind could imagine.

Go.

In a bathroom that wasn't hers. With a toilet she didn't trust. And a history I couldn't see.

And afterward, as I helped her wash her hands and dry her face, she looked up at me with something like relief and something like disbelief.

From then on, that's how we did it.

Every unfamiliar bathroom. Every trip outside our home.

She had to be held tightly, securely the entire time on the toilet. Not rushed. Not left to manage it alone. My neck wrapped with her arms became her anchor in those moments, the thing that told her: This time, no one will hurt you.

* * *

But if I moved at all, loosening her grip, even just a little, she'd panic. Her eyes would flash with the old fear, and the cries would begin again.

It took a long time before we could even think of backing away. A long time before the sight of a strange bathroom didn't send her spiraling. But we kept holding her. Again and again and again.

Her fear wasn't logical. It was deep and visceral. That kind of fear doesn't come from nowhere. Whatever had happened in her past, being physically held seemed to help her body believe she was safe.

Over time, we slowly helped her build confidence. First, we held her close. Then just her hands. Eventually, we could stand nearby without touching at all. But it took years. It was years of patient reassurance before she could use the bathroom without fear gripping her.

We'll likely never know the full story behind why bathrooms triggered her so intensely. But we do know her older half-sister entered a bathroom once with their birth mother and came out with a permanent injury.

Her older half-sister has a prominent limp from time spent alone in a bathroom with her birth mother. Nothing good happened in bathrooms with that woman. We don't know exactly what happened, but we've learned this much: for our kids, bathrooms had been places of fear. Places of danger.

Judy was terrified of the dark. Bedtime wasn't loud or chaotic, but it was a silent war. She didn't tantrum or act out. She just refused to sleep. She would lie perfectly still, eyes wide open, staring at the ceiling for hours. It wasn't stubbornness; it was fear.

Something in her small body refused to surrender to sleep, as though she believed that closing her eyes would invite danger. Even in the safety of her own bed, surrounded by the quiet rhythms of a home that loved her, she couldn't let her guard down.

Night after night, we watched the same routine play out. It wasn't until deep in the night, when exhaustion finally overcame her, that her little body would give in to sleep. The darkness wasn't empty for her. It was haunted by memories, or perhaps just the ghost of what had once been terrifyingly real.

Judy was also terrified of grass and bugs. Given her early experiences, her fear of insects, especially after what she endured with cockroaches, made sense. But her fear extended beyond what most would expect. She wasn't just scared of the unpleasant kind of bugs. She was afraid of all insects.

It was a warm afternoon. The kind where the sun poured through the windshield in golden waves and the car hummed with quiet contentment. We were parked in the grocery store lot, waiting for curbside pickup. Judy was in her car seat behind me, legs swinging, half singing, half mumbling to herself.

Then, a butterfly landed on the passenger-side window.

It was small and delicate. Its wings soft with color, paper-thin and flickering in the light. I smiled at it.

"Look, Judy," I said, turning slightly in my seat. "A butterfly!"

But the moment her eyes landed on it, everything changed.

She screamed.

A high, sharp wail exploded from the back seat, raw and panicked, as if she were being attacked. Her hands flew up, covering her face, then flailed in the air as if she could swat the fear itself away.

"No! No! Get it away! GET IT AWAY!" she shrieked, pressing her body against the opposite door, trying to climb up and out of her car seat.

"Judy, honey, it's okay," I said quickly, heart racing. "It's just a butterfly. It's outside the car. It can't hurt you."

She couldn't hear me over her own sobbing. Her whole body was shaking, fists clenched, eyes wild with terror. Tears streamed down her cheeks as she let out another scream, louder this time, more primal. I reached back and touched her leg gently.

"I promise, it can't get to you. Look," I pointed. "It's on the outside. It's just resting on the glass."

"Noooo!" she screamed, thrashing wildly as if trying to fight off something only she could see. Her arms flailed, clawing at the air, and her legs kicked. She twisted away from everything and everyone, curling into herself like she was trying to escape a nightmare that had spilled into daylight.

I wish I had responded with tenderness. I wish I had pulled the car over, unbuckled her, pulled her into my lap, and rocked her until the storm passed. That would've been the right response.

But by then, it had been years of trauma, years of meltdowns over the smallest things, years of being screamed at, bitten, peed on, pooped on, worn down to my bones by Manny, Gio, and her. I was frayed, exhausted, and on edge.

I didn't respond like the mother I wanted to be.

"It's just a butterfly," I snapped. "Stop screaming. You'll wake the baby."

Even as the words left my mouth, guilt swelled in my chest. I knew better. I knew this wasn't about the butterfly. This was about whatever horror her body remembered when she saw something with wings. This was trauma, not defiance. As each day of trauma wore me a little more I lost more of myself, of the mom I had been before they came into our home.

I softened, finally. My voice lowered as I looked back at her flailing in her car seat.

"I'm sorry," I whispered, guilty tears stinging my eyes. "It's not going to come in. You're safe. I'm here."

My dwindling patience with her and her continued massive meltdowns both broke my heart. The thing outside the window was so fragile, so harmless, so beautiful and yet it had triggered a storm inside her that I couldn't calm.

When the butterfly finally lifted off and drifted away, her screams quieted to sobs, then hiccups, and then a low, fearful whimper.

"I don't like it," she said, voice trembling.

"I know, sweet girl," I said more gently this time. "You don't have to like it. I'll protect you. Always."

She didn't ask questions. Didn't explain. Just sat there trembling, holding my hand as I drove until her breath evened out.

Whatever that butterfly reminded her of, it wasn't light or softness.

It was something darker. Something deep.

No words could reach her in those moments. She was completely overtaken by a fear so intense it left her paralyzed. These episodes made simple outings incredibly challenging. A trip to the park or even a fast-food restaurant could quickly unravel.

If a fly happened to buzz by, she would have a full-blown meltdown. To onlookers, it likely looked like I had a group of completely out-of-control children: Manny, silent and expressionless, made to stay by my side; Gio, quick to lash out at any child who came too close; and Judy, screaming in terror over something as small as an insect.

The judgment from others was fierce, and once again, it led to more isolation. There was no such thing as a simple family outing. Every time we tried, chaos followed. People didn't see the trauma behind the behaviors; they only saw a mom with 'unruly' kids, and the looks we got made it easier just to stay home. But what they didn't know was that these children weren't misbehaving. They were surviving.

Judy also liked to boss her younger siblings. It became one of her early ways of asserting control in a world that had once made her feel powerless. She took charge of games, assigned roles, enforced rules whether the others liked it or not. At times, it made the other kids roll their eyes or push back, but beneath the bossiness was something familiar: a little girl trying to prove she was safe by staying in charge.

If she was the one directing the play, maybe she wouldn't feel so vulnerable. And the truth is, she wasn't always wrong. She often had a sense of what would go wrong before it did. Her instincts were sharp. She had survived by staying alert, and now she was practicing that same vigilance in the playroom.

It started with nothing.

Or at least, nothing I could see.

Judy was six. She was small for her age, wiry, all legs and tension. We'd just come home from the park. She'd had a snack, her favorite show was on, and everything seemed fine. Ordinary.

And then, like a switch flipped, she exploded.

One second, she was sitting on the couch. The next, she was screaming. Loud, guttural, terrified.

"No!" she shrieked, flinging a pillow across the room. "No! Don't touch me! Don't look at me!"

I stood quickly. "Judy, what's wrong? What happened?"

She didn't answer. Just kept screaming, face red, eyes wild, fists clenched so tight her knuckles turned white. Then came the kicking, the punching, arms flailing in every direction, as if she were trying to fight off an invisible enemy. Her fear wasn't performative. It was raw. Animal. Out of her control.

And if I didn't step in, she could hurt herself. Or someone else.

So I did the only thing I could.

I dropped to the floor beside her and gently wrapped my arms around her in what therapists call a "therapeutic hold" : a firm, secure hug designed to keep a child from spiraling into harm. It wasn't forceful. It wasn't punishment. It was safety. Containment. A steady, calm, I've got you in the middle of a hurricane.

She thrashed. She screamed in my ear. "LET GO! LET GO!"

My heart cracked, but I didn't flinch.

"I'm here," I whispered. "You're safe. I'm not going to let you hurt yourself. I'm not letting go until you're safe."

"I SAID GO AWAY!" she howled, trying to claw her way out of my grip trying to scratch and inflict pain on me so I would let go.

Her body jolted against mine again and again, writhing with rage or was it fear? Maybe both. I kept my voice soft, steady. I slowed my breathing so she could feel it. A metronome. A lifeline.

"I've got you, baby girl. You're not alone."

Minutes passed. Ten. Twenty. Thirty.

And then, just as suddenly as it began, her body softened.

Her fists unclenched. Her legs stopped kicking. Her breath came in short, broken sobs, and her head dropped to my shoulder like she couldn't hold it up anymore.

"I've got you," I said again, brushing her damp hair from her face.

She didn't speak for a moment.

Then, through the tears, she whispered, voice small and shaking, "I want you to keep me safe."

My arms tightened instinctively.

"I'm scared," she said, pressing her face to my neck. "And I need you."

I didn't answer with words. Just rocked her. Slowly. Steadily.

* * *

It was the kind of raw, honest cry that most adults can't admit out loud. She was only six, and I don't think she even fully understood what she was feeling, but in that moment, she let it surface. Beneath all the anger, beneath the noise and chaos, there was fear. And a quiet, desperate hope that someone might be strong enough to hold her through it.

Judy came to us carrying fears too big for her tiny body: fears of bathrooms, of darkness, of sleep, of bugs, of being out of control. And yet, day by day, she let herself be loved through them. She didn't heal all at once; she learned safety in layers. A meltdown held in arms that wouldn't let go. A whispered cry for help that didn't go unanswered.

Her story wasn't about instant transformation. It was about a child slowly learning that love didn't leave, that safety could be real, and that the world could hold something gentler than what she had known. And with every small victory, Judy reclaimed a piece of her childhood, not erased, but redeemed.

Lessons in the Wilderness

Judy's story is a tender reminder that sometimes the wilderness isn't just a place outside; it is the place inside a heart, a dark and lonely terrain filled with fears no one else can see. The wilderness of trauma can feel endless, cold, and frightening, and the scars it leaves are invisible but deep.

Yet, it is in this wilderness that God's presence is most faithful. When the fears press in, when the meltdowns come like storms, and when the past's shadows threaten to overwhelm, God remains the steadfast anchor.

God does not promise an instant miracle or the swift erasing of pain. Instead, He offers His patient love which is strong enough to hold us when we cannot stand, gentle enough to calm our trembling hearts, and steady enough to carry us through each small step forward.

Judy's healing came in slow layers, moments of safety held tight in arms that refused to let go. It is in those quiet, broken moments that

God's grace works, teaching us to trust again. God meets us in our fragility and whispers, "I am with you. You are not alone."

For those who walk through the wilderness, whether children or adults, God's promise is sure: the desert will bloom, the night will give way to dawn, and even the deepest wounds can be redeemed by His unfailing love.

May we lean into His presence, trusting that He who holds Judy so tenderly holds us as well.

"The LORD your God is in your midst,
  a mighty one who will save;
  he will rejoice over you with gladness;
  he will quiet you by his love;
  he will exult over you with loud singing."
  — Zephaniah 3:17 (ESV)

Prayer:
       Father God, thank You that You meet us in the wilderness inside our hearts and in the hidden places of pain. When fear and sorrow feel overwhelming, be our steady anchor and gentle comfort. Help us to trust Your patient love that never lets go, and to believe that healing comes one small step at a time. Surround every wounded heart with Your peace and remind us that You rejoice over us with gladness. In Jesus' name, Amen.

8

This was the darkest season of my life. I couldn't see a way forward. Every morning I woke up with a pit in my stomach, knowing I had at least another decade ahead of me raising Manny.

It didn't feel like motherhood anymore; it felt like a sentence. A life confined to constant vigilance, constant fear. There were no signs of improvement, only deeper descent into danger. Danger I successfully was protecting the other kids in the home from, but in doing so I was losing my joy.

What made it worse was that no one truly saw what was happening in our home. No one saw how terrifying Manny could be. How calculated and how crue he was, especially toward the other children. And toward me. We were utterly alone in it. People assumed he was just a troubled kid who needed more love. But I had poured every ounce of love I had into him. It wasn't enough. It was never going to be enough.

And it wasn't just the predatory behavior I had to be on constant guard against. It was his growing appetite for cruelty. He liked hurting animals. That's not an exaggeration. I couldn't let him play in the backyard without supervision. I'd try to juggle time between the younger kids inside and giving Manny space to burn off energy outside.

It always happened when I stepped away.

* * *

Just for a moment. Into the kitchen to grab a glass of water, or outside to check the laundry on the line. I'd glance through the window, see the dog sniffing the grass, and I'd tell myself, It's fine. Just a minute.

But then I'd hear it.

A sharp yelp, high-pitched and sudden, cutting through the summer air like a warning bell.

Then came the blur of fur, our dog bolting across the yard, tail tucked low, ears pinned back, scrambling for safety. Sometimes under the porch. Sometimes behind the garbage bins. Anywhere she could get away.

And there was Manny.

Standing where the dog had been moments ago. Face unreadable. Sometimes holding a stick. Sometimes empty-handed. But always too still. Too calm.

"Manny," I'd call, trying to keep my voice steady as I stepped back outside. "What happened?"

"She wouldn't listen," he'd say, eyes following the dog as she cowered in the corner of the yard. "She ran away from me."

I knew that look on the dog's face with her whole body trembling, eyes wide, ribs moving fast with each breath. That wasn't the fear of a game gone wrong. That was the fear of pain. Of being trapped. Of not knowing what would come next.

Just like Manny had once felt.

And now, he was passing it on.

That was the hardest part. Watching him turn his own scars outward and even the dog wasn't exempt. This was a big dog, too. It was gentle, protective, and strong. But he was terrified of Manny. And that terrified me.

* * *

I remember one morning, standing in the kitchen, looking out the window into the yard. We had chickens at the time, just a small backyard flock, and I had thought maybe giving Manny some simple farm chores might help him. Something structured. Grounding. Good. Each morning, I'd lock up the dog and send him out with his egg basket, hoping the responsibility would be something he could take pride in.

That day, I stood at the window, watching. Manny didn't know I was there. He walked across the yard toward the coop, holding the basket carefully. But then I saw it. His eyes flicked toward the rocking chair on the porch. The one I usually sat in when I supervised him outside. He was checking. Testing.

When he thought no one was watching, a slow, crooked smile spread across his face.

I didn't know what was coming, but I knew that look. I'd seen it before. The glint in his eyes when he believed he could act without consequence.

He set the basket down on the grass.

And then, he ran at the chickens. Full speed. Lashing out with his feet.

It took me a second to register what I was seeing. The flurry of feathers, the panicked squawks, the unfiltered glee on his face. It wasn't frustration. It wasn't a child losing control. It was pleasure. He was enjoying it.

My stomach dropped. I rushed outside, yelling his name, but the chickens were already scattered, terrified. One stumbled away, clearly injured.

That moment was seared into my mind. I stood at the window, breath caught, heart pounding, not just from what I'd seen, but from what it meant.

It stripped away any last hope I had that this was just a phase and just trauma he could grow out of. There was something much darker at play.

He wasn't out of control. He was in control and he liked hurting things when no one was looking. That was the moment I stopped believing he could change.

In my shock, it took a second for me to react, but then instinct kicked in. I threw open the door and ran outside, screaming his name.

He was mid-kick when he froze, hearing me. One of the chickens had collapsed and lay motionless in the dirt. I called him to come to me.

He turned slowly, his little fists clenched tight at his sides, his face twisted in rage. I asked, trying to stay calm, "Why were you kicking the chickens?"

With burning eyes, he shouted back, "I wasn't!"

His voice was full of fury, not fear. I reminded him gently, "Manny, I saw you. I was watching from the window. You saw me when I yelled your name."

But there was no apology, no flicker of remorse. Only defiance. Even caught in the act, he refused to admit what he had done. The truth was irrelevant. He was consumed with rage, so determined to reject any authority or accountability, that he stood there shaking with hate.

I could feel it coming off of him hot and suffocating. I'd seen anger before, from toddlers and teenagers alike, but this was something different. This was a hatred that felt directed at me not because of what I said, but because I had seen through his mask of charm he liked to hide behind.

His face moved closer to mine, his body tight like a coiled spring. I could tell things were escalating fast, so I lowered my voice and told him calmly, "Go to your room."

He stormed off without a word.

A few minutes later, I checked on him. What I found left me stunned.

In a deliberate act of defiance and spite, he had urinated on nearly every item in his room: his clothes, his toys, even the walls. Then he had defecated on himself and sat in it, smearing it across the bed as if to say, I will destroy anything you give me.

It wasn't a meltdown. It wasn't a cry for help. It was calculated, intentional.

And I stood in the doorway exhausted, heartbroken, and utterly lost, realizing just how deeply broken things had become.

This was my daily life for years with Manny.

Extreme behaviors. Lying even when caught red-handed. And then, as if on cue, soiling himself in anger whenever he was confronted.

The pattern became predictable. I'd catch him doing something harmful, he'd deny it, no matter how clear the evidence, then lash out by destroying something or making himself filthy, as if to punish me for seeing the truth.

Fire became another fixation. We began finding burnt objects hidden in corners of the yard. Lighters and matches stashed in toy bins or his coat pockets. I had to start searching his backpack and clothes every day before and after school. Anything that could ignite something had to be locked up or hidden.

He loved setting things on fire. There was something in it that thrilled him watching things burn, watching destruction happen.

It started with a low crackle so faint I almost missed it.

Then the sirens came.

I stepped out the front door and froze.

Across the street, the old barn was engulfed in flames. Towering pillars of fire shot into the sky, turning the evening light orange. Thick black smoke curled into the clouds like a living thing, choking out the sun.

* * *

And there was Manny.

Standing at our fence.

Just… watching.

He didn't move. Didn't flinch. The fire raged, and he stood like a statue: calm, still, with a faint smile creeping across his face. Not wild or giddy, just… satisfied. Like the flames were something he understood.

I felt my stomach flip.

I sprinted toward him, heart pounding. "Manny! Why didn't you come get me?!" I yelled.

He turned slowly. His eyes met mine with a strange kind of softness.

And he smiled.

Not with guilt. Not with fear.

Just smiled.

I couldn't breathe. There was no evidence. No matches in his pocket, no soot on his hands. But my gut twisted hard. My body knew what I didn't want to admit.

Something was wrong.

Something had been wrong for a long time.

And that sick, crawling dread, that knot in my stomach that whispered, this isn't normal, became a permanent part of me from that day forward. Like a warning bell I couldn't unring.

I never proved anything. But I never forgot that smile.

That moment watching the fire, watching him… it felt like a metaphor for everything. Not just the danger, but how, in choosing to love him, we lit a match that burned through everything good we had. My biological children were drowning under the weight of dysfunction Manny had brought to our home. In adopting Manny I had taken fire to the healthy family unit we once enjoyed.

With each big destructive event there was no certainty it was him. No evidence that anyone could see. Just a thousand moments like that one: quiet, chilling, and unmistakably real to me.

I was completely defeated. I didn't know how to fix this. There was no parenting book, no advice, no therapist, and no prayer that seemed to make a dent anymore.

After the fire incident, I called Manny inside and told him to go to his room. Minutes later, the now-familiar pattern repeated: out of rage, he soiled himself...and the room.

When I walked in, the smell hit first. Then I saw it, smeared across the floor, on the walls, and on his bed. I grabbed a paper towel, picked up a piece of feces, and held it in the paper towel as I asked him, exhausted and numb, "Why did you do this? The bathroom is literally right across the hall."

He stared at me, completely straight-faced, and said, "I didn't do it."

It was staggering. This moment of utter defiance, of complete disconnection from reality. I stood there, holding the literal evidence, and he looked me in the eye and denied everything.

By then, Manny had his own room for safety reasons. No one else could have done it. The bathroom was steps away. Still, he stared at me and calmly and coldly said, "I didn't do it."

It wasn't just lying. It was detachment from reality itself like trying to reason with a hurricane. You can't. You can only run away from its destruction or hunker down and wait it out and pray the destruction is not too great.

I left his room defeated and quietly closed the door behind me. I didn't yell. I didn't cry. I just walked down the hallway in silence and stepped into my bedroom right next door to his. I stood there for a long time in front of the mirror, staring at my own reflection like I was looking at a stranger.

Who was this woman? The one with the tired eyes, the slumped shoulders, the hollow face. All the joy, all the color in me, felt drained out. I couldn't remember what it felt like to be light. To feel hope.

I stood there and began to question everything. Everything.

Was that really God's voice we heard when we felt called to adopt? Had we misunderstood? Surely God wouldn't lead us down a road this brutal, this confusing, this isolating. Surely obedience wasn't supposed to cost this much.

Then the darker questions crept in. How would I survive this? How could I keep doing this for years to come?

There were other children in my home: beautiful, innocent children who deserved laughter, safety, joy. But I was giving everything I had just to keep the house from burning down, emotionally and sometimes almost literally.

I felt like I was spending every day putting out emotional fires, scrambling from one blaze to the next, never able to breathe, never able to rebuild. Manny took up so much of my attention, so much of my energy, that I started to wonder if I had anything left to give the rest of my family. They were getting scraps.

And that terrified me.

How could I give them a joyful childhood while living in survival mode? I was consumed with guilt, not just over how hard it was, but over how far I had drifted from the kind of mother I once was. I didn't recognize my life anymore. I didn't recognize myself anymore.

And there, in that moment, in that mirror, I began to grieve, not just for Manny's story, but for mine too.

I was the house on fire. And no one was coming to put it out.

* * *

With Manny, I sometimes had glimmers of hope. He would suddenly seem to turn a corner working hard, behaving well, showing moments of sweetness that made me believe we were finally getting through. I wanted so badly to believe he was changing. That he was healing.

But every time it happened, I'd eventually discover that he'd just been trying to earn back my trust so he could hide something darker. Some new scheme. Some terrible behavior I hadn't yet uncovered. I started calling these stretches "flying under the radar." Because that's exactly what they were: calculated periods of calm that always came before the storm.

Still, I soaked up those rare quiet moments knowing, yet needing to believe. I needed them. They were the only breaths I got from the chaos that had become my life.

In the very beginning, before the cracks started to show, Manny would sit in my lap for hours. I'd pull him close, his small body stiff at first, like he didn't know how to relax into love. We'd settle in at the kitchen table, books and math worksheets spread out between us. I'd wrap my arms around him while we worked. He was years behind. He couldn't read simple words, didn't understand basic numbers. But I didn't mind.

I told myself: This is what healing looks like. Quiet, consistent presence. One lesson, one hug, one soft word at a time.

I believed we were bonding. That each moment spent sounding out syllables or solving two plus two was stitching something back together inside him. I believed that love, poured out daily in that little chair, would be enough.

And for a little while, it looked like it might be. He smiled sometimes. He laughed at silly stories. He leaned against me with a weight that felt like trust.

Now I look back and wonder, was any of that real? Or was it just part of the mask? Another part of the performance?

* * *

And if it was real, why wasn't it enough? Maybe it never could be. But I know this: I was there. I showed up. Every day, I stayed in the fire.

Lessons in the Wilderness

There are seasons in life when the wilderness feels like a burning house: chaos all around, smoke choking hope, and no clear way out. For myself, those years with Manny were exactly that kind of wilderness: a place of relentless fire, fear, and heartbreak, where every day felt like survival.

When pain and struggle surround us, it's easy to feel abandoned, isolated, and utterly defeated. The weight of the unseen battles, those hidden wounds and relentless storms, can crush even the strongest spirit. Sometimes, we find ourselves staring in the mirror, questioning everything: Who am I now? Where is the God who called me to this? How long must I stay in this fire?

The wilderness is often where our faith is tested most fiercely. It is where God's voice can seem distant, and His promises feel heavy with silence. Yet even in that desert of doubt and despair, God is present. Sometimes not to immediately rescue us from the flames, but to carry us through them.

When the fire feels too hot to bear, when the burden of love seems beyond our strength, we can cling to the truth that God is with us, holding us steady. His grace is sufficient even when our hope falters, His strength made perfect in our weakness.

My story with Manny reminds us that obedience and love do not guarantee smooth paths. Sometimes the call to love means walking through the fiercest fires, step by painful step. But God never leaves us in the flames alone. His promise is that He will be our refuge, our shield, our safe place in the storm.

In the wilderness, healing may seem distant and change invisible. But God's work is often quiet, slow, and unseen. Every day we show up and every moment we choose love instead of giving up, God is stitching grace into the scorched places of our hearts.

* * *

If you find yourself in your own wilderness today, take heart. The night is darkest just before dawn. Hold on to the God who promises to never leave you, who can turn even the fiercest fires into a refining grace.

"The LORD is my light and my salvation; whom shall I fear?
The LORD is the stronghold of my life; of whom shall I be afraid?"
— Psalm 27:1 (ESV)

Prayer:

Lord, in the midst of my wilderness, when the fire rages and hope feels distant, remind me that You are my refuge and strength. Carry me through the flames when I am too weak to walk alone. Help me to trust Your presence even when the way is hard and the healing seems slow. Fill me with Your peace and grace, and shape my heart by Your loving hand. Thank You for never leaving me, even in the darkest night. In Jesus' name, Amen.

9

Parenting a child who comes from trauma means loving before you understand. It means showing up day after day with open hands and a soft heart, even when your trust is broken and your patience is gone.

With Gio, everything was a first. Firsts he should have had as a toddler, not a five-year-old. First time hearing about God. First time using the bathroom the right way. First time being told "no" and not being afraid that meant abandonment. He had survived so much by the time he came to us, and now survival had to give way to something gentler. But survival doesn't let go easily.

Gio never woke up planning to do the wrong thing. His biggest struggles weren't born from defiance, but from a mind shaped by trauma and a body still healing from what was done before he ever had a chance.

He wasn't malicious; he was impulsive. Quick to act, slow to think, and often unaware of the ripple his choices would cause. Like so many children whose beginnings were marked by prenatal drug and alcohol exposure, Gio's wiring made life harder for him in ways even he couldn't understand. And it made parenting him a daily exercise in grace, patience, and the constant prayer: Lord, help me see the difference between sin and brokenness.

Raising him often felt like trying to parent someone caught in a current they couldn't see but were always swept away by. It was hard to know what was willful disobedience and what was a brain that just couldn't keep up. One of the most constant battles was with food. Gio struggled deeply with impulse control around eating constantly sneaking snacks, hiding wrappers, and raiding cabinets in the night.

One year, I stocked up on Christmas candy during the after-holiday sales, tucking away six kids stockings' worth for the next year. Days later, I found Gio sitting quietly in a room, sitting quietly, knees pulled in, surrounded by a sea of silver and red wrappers. All of it, every last piece, had been unwrapped and eaten. It wasn't rebellion. It wasn't even selfishness. It was his trauma and wiring, playing out again. And I just stood there in the doorway, holding both frustration and compassion in the same breath.

I had to do daily checks of his room, his backpack, and all the hidden corners he claimed as his own. Gio hoarded food like his survival depended on it because, at one point in his life, it had. His hunger wasn't just for calories; it was for safety, for control, for a reassurance that he wouldn't go without again. Every time I tried to talk to him about healthy portions or eating in moderation, it landed like a punishment. I could see it in his eyes. Some deep part of him was being reminded of the days when there simply wasn't enough.

Teaching him healthy habits became one of the most emotionally complicated tasks I faced. His biological family struggled with extreme obesity, and I knew I had to fight for his long-term health. But how do you teach balance without triggering a child who came from starvation? We did our best with what we could.

His eating habits had already begun to take a toll on his health. By the time he came to us, his teeth were in a heartbreaking state and were completely blackened and beyond saving. At just four years old, he had to have six teeth removed. The damage had been done long before we met him, a result of poor hygiene habits and a diet that had lacked any guidance or restraint. The dentist gave me a stern lecture, assuming I had let him consume too many gummies and too much apple juice. I didn't bother explaining. I had grown weary of constantly justifying myself, tired of repeating that I wasn't the one who had let his teeth rot.

I created an 'anytime snack bowl,' filled with nutritious, tasty options.

It sat on the table like a promise: You'll never go hungry again. He could eat from it freely, no permission needed. But junk food still had rules, and that led to battles. His trauma collided with our love.

It wasn't rebellion. It wasn't defiance. It was survival instinct in a child who hadn't yet been taught there was another way.

In those early years, I often felt like a missionary to my own child sent to a land of deep wounds, speaking a language of love he didn't yet understand.

It wasn't that Gio wouldn't do things the right way; he simply didn't know how. Gio also struggled with bathroom issues, but they weren't like Manny's. His challenges weren't rooted in malice or mental illness. They were simply the result of years of neglect and poor teaching. Nearly five years of life without consistent guidance or hygiene training had left their mark.

Gio would use whatever bathroom was closest or sometimes none at all. He didn't understand why it mattered. Convenience, urgency, confusion… it was hard to tell what guided his choices.

Then one day, a strange odor began drifting through the house.

It wasn't the normal kind of "boy smell." It was heavier. Rank. And no matter how much I scrubbed, it lingered.

I sprayed. I mopped. I checked trash cans. I washed sheets. Still, the smell haunted the air like a secret.

That evening, I walked through the hall with my nose crinkled, determined to track it down. As I passed Gio's room, a strong wave of it hit me like a punch in the face.

"Oh no," I whispered.

I knelt beside the air vent near his bed and took off the cover.

My heart dropped.

* * *

Inside, stuffed deep, was a mass of soiled underwear, tissues… and feces. Human feces.

"Gio!" I called, my voice sharper than I intended. "Come here right now!"

He came slowly, eyes uncertain.

I pointed at the vent. "Do you know anything about this?"

He paused, shifting from foot to foot. "I didn't go on the bed," he said defensively, avoiding my eyes.

I blinked, caught off guard by the answer. "You… you didn't go on the bed?"

He nodded. "I know I'm not supposed to. So I put it in there. So you wouldn't see."

There it was.

Not defiance. Not laziness. Shame. Fear. Survival instincts shaped by years of chaos.

I sat down on the edge of the bed, suddenly exhausted.

"Sweetheart," I said, "You need to use a bathroom. You can't just go wherever you want."

He stared at the vent. "I didn't want you to be mad if I got out of my room after bedtime."

My throat tightened.

"I'm won't be mad at you having to go to the bathroom, Gio." I said, even though part of me wanted to scream at the absurdity and sadness of it all. "I'm just… really sorry someone taught you to hide things like that."

He didn't answer. Just stood there, arms crossed over his chest like armor.

Once I discovered the hidden feces, I checked his room more thoroughly. I found that he had been using the curtains to wipe, and worse, he had peed inside his dresser drawers making every shirt and pants inside soaking wet with urine. He had even peed in his toy box. It wasn't spiteful; it was survival, habit, confusion. Walking to the bathroom simply hadn't been part of his early life. Hygiene had never been modeled or enforced.

Later, I heard a story about his birth mother that helped me understand more deeply just how foreign the idea of hygiene had been in Gio's early world.

In a moment of raw anger toward her boyfriend, she chose a revolting act of revenge: she defecated on his phone, in front of everyone, right there in the middle of the living room.

That's the world Gio came from. That was the norm he had to unlearn. And he did unlearn it. He started flushing the toilet without reminders. He stopped asking if he'd still get dinner tomorrow. The little things that showed something had shifted.

When the heater kicked on later that night, the stench rolled through the vents and the house like a haunting reminder. Not just of what had happened, but of what this little boy had survived and how much still needed to be unlearned.

Slowly, patiently, painfully he learned. He healed.

Lessons in the Wilderness

Parenting a child marked by trauma calls us to walk a narrow path of faith: one that requires loving before we fully understand and showing up day after day with hands open and hearts softened, even when our patience wears thin and trust feels broken.

The Apostle Paul reminds us, *"Be completely humble and gentle; be patient, bearing with one another in love"* (Ephesians 4:2). I have failed at this more times that I care to admit, but each morning I brushed off my impatience from the day before and tried again to live out this command from scripture.

This is the calling God places on us, not just to love when it's easy, but to love through the hardest, messiest seasons. When we face behaviors we cannot control or comprehend, when progress feels slow or absent, our faith is tested.

Like the Israelites wandering the wilderness, we may feel lost, weary, and unsure if the promised land of healing will ever come. Sometimes, as with Gio, healing comes very slowly. Sometimes, like with Manny, it never comes at all. Yet God's word assures us: "I will never leave you nor forsake you" (Hebrews 13:5). When the road seems endless and hope fragile, God's presence is our constant.

Loving a child shaped by trauma means trusting God to do what we cannot. It means praying with persistence for wisdom and strength, as James encourages: *"If any of you lacks wisdom, you should ask God, who gives generously to all without finding fault"* (James 1:5). We ask, not for easy answers, but for grace to walk patiently through each challenge.

When we are tempted to despair at the wilderness pressing in on us at every side, the Psalmist's words can renew our spirit:

"The Lord is close to the brokenhearted and saves those who are crushed in spirit" (Psalm 34:18).

Your daily acts of love, showing up again, and offering kindness when met with defiance are never wasted. They are prayers in action, seeds planted in the wilderness. God sees every step, every sacrifice, every moment you choose to stay and love. Remember, you aren't living for this life, you are living for eternity. That eternal perspective bring peace in the midst of a chaotic life.

In the quiet, in the struggle, and in the waiting God is at work. He is shaping you and your child. Lean into Him. Trust His timing. And keep loving, even when it feels like a desert.

If you feel like the wilderness is endless, hold on to this promise:

* * *

"For I know the plans I have for you," declares the Lord, "plans to prosper you and not to harm you, plans to give you hope and a future" (Jeremiah 29:11).

Prayer:

Father, thank You for Your unfailing presence in the wilderness seasons of parenting. When patience runs thin and hope feels fragile, remind me that You never leave or forsake me. Give me wisdom to walk this narrow path of love with humility and gentleness. Strengthen my heart to keep showing up, keep loving, and keep trusting Your perfect plans. Help me to see beyond today's struggle to the hope and future You have promised. In Jesus' name, Amen

10

Some things we expect from childhood, like breathing, eating, and sleeping, to happen without instruction. But smiling and laughing? Those sometimes have to be learned. For Judy and her brothers, joy was an unfamiliar language: something they'd watched but never spoken.

In the early days, capturing family moments felt bittersweet, because in every photo I saw evidence of what their childhood had been denied. From Judy, I learned that you can undo the deprivation of joy in their early years. Joy can be taught, nurtured, and, in time, become as natural as breathing.

From the moment they arrived, the first sign of needing to teach joy played out in our photo sessions. I'd gather the kids, hold up my phone, and say cheerfully, "Okay, everyone, say cheese!" My biological children would grin freely, eyes crinkling at the corners. Gio might manage a polite half-smile. But Judy and Manny? Their faces froze as though I'd asked them to recite a foreign alphabet.

They contorted their mouths into tight, puzzled grimaces, trying to guess what a smile should look like. Those strained expressions, mouths curled in unfamiliar shapes, reminded me that joy had never been whispered to their souls. Instead of laughter echoing around the room, there was silence and confusion.

A single photo could tell a thousand stories. In one family portrait that used to hang on my living room wall, Manny stands rigid with eyes wide, arms at his sides; Gio's cheeks are tight, the expression halfway between a smile and a wince; and Judy, sweet Judy, has her lips pressed together so firmly that her small nose wrinkles, as though she's trying to force a shape she does not yet know. In that picture, their eyes betray them: shadows of fear, uncertainty, and the weight of things no child should bear.

Teaching them to smile felt like building a bridge over a canyon they had grown up knowing only as a void. I began by making them watch themselves in the mirror. On one Saturday morning, I lined us up in front of a full-length mirror.

I stood behind each child, placing a hand gently on their shoulder. "Look here," I said, and demonstrated a natural, relaxed smile: the corners of my mouth rising, my cheeks lifting, eyes brightening. Then I asked them to try.

Gio studied my face, his lips twitching as he tried to mimic the upward curve. He managed a tentative wobble of a grin before his cheeks fell back to a flat line. I praised his effort, "Good job! Just like that!" and guided him again: "A little higher at the corners. Pretend you just saw your favorite ice cream." With each encouragement, his lips inched upward, and even though his eyes still held a flicker of confusion, he learned to trace the pattern until the shape felt less foreign.

Judy was a bit more eager. She tilted her head and studied my reflection, blue eyes bright under her curly lashes. "Like this?" she asked, poking at the corners of her mouth. I nodded, and gently molded her face: "Yes, exactly. Now let the corners lift without thinking, just feel happy."

She tried that, too, and I saw relief wash over her face when her eyes brightened just a fraction. Each day after, I'd catch her practicing in the bathroom mirror before bed. In those moments, I realized how fragile hope could be, but also how resilient a child's spirit is when given permission to heal.

While smiles could be guided with hands and mirrors, laughter was a different puzzle. I recall one evening when the whole family gathered on the couch to watch a silly cartoon. My biological kids giggled naturally; their little knees bounced. Gio managed a polite chuckle once he recognized the sound it was making. But Judy, she studied our faces, trying to identify what a laugh sounded like. Eventually, with determination in her eyes, she let out a loud, high-pitched staccato: "HAAA-HA! HAA-HA!"

It wasn't laughter in the way I knew, but it was her first attempt at speaking that joyful language. The sound was awkward, shocking, and untuned, but she meant it to be happy.

Her laugh often came at the wrong times. She would burst into uncontrollable giggles when someone got hurt, or when a character in a movie was crying. It wasn't cruel. It was never mockery. It was a deep disconnection. It was her brain reaching for the one emotion that felt "safe" rather than confronting anything that made her feel vulnerable.

I remember when she was six and broke her leg on the little trampoline in our basement. We heard laughter coming from downstairs. It was a wild, manic laughter. I went to check on her. She was sitting on the floor, unable to stand, laughing like she had just heard the best joke of her life. But each time she tried to put weight on her leg, her laughter intensified, like her body didn't know how else to respond.

We had never seen a child laugh instead of cry when in pain. It was so unexpected that it took us a full day to realize her leg was actually broken. We kept thinking, If it were really serious, she'd be in tears. We didn't yet understand that even at that young age, she had already learned to mask her pain in a costume of manic laughter.

That pattern hasn't fully disappeared with age. Even now, as an adult, she struggles with allowing herself to feel pain openly. Just recently, when she sprained her ankle, she laughed every time her father tried to wrap it or put ice on it. She'd be sitting quietly in bed, then suddenly start giggling. Each laugh was triggered not by something funny, but by discomfort she didn't know how to express.

Letting others see her hurt still feels dangerous to her. Needing help feels unsafe. So she defaults to laughter. It's the emotion that asks nothing of anyone and shields everything underneath. But she's growing. Bit by bit, she's learning that it's okay to cry. That it's okay to need someone. That pain doesn't always have to be hidden behind a smile.

When she was young in our home, I seized every opportunity to guide her. During tickle fights, I'd lightly tickle her sides, then pause and encourage her: "Can you try to make a happy sound like my laugh? That's it. Let it come out." She tried, voice trembling until laughter tremored through her.

I'll never forget the day Judy burst into tears and said, "No one likes my laugh." I had taken her to the park, where children chased bubbles in the golden afternoon. A dad behind us played peekaboo with his toddler, and genuine laughter filled the air. I glanced at Judy and saw her cheeks wet with tears as she tried to join the chorus but felt visibly out of place. She looked up at me and cried, "They're staring at me."

I held her, rocking back and forth. "I love your laugh," I whispered, "but maybe we can practice together. We'll make it sweet, just like you are." She nodded, wiping her face. In the shade of a big oak tree, we slowly worked through giggles. First quiet, then louder. She tried variations until the laughter that emerged felt more like hers.

On the walk home, she pulled my hand and whispered, "I like to laugh, mom." By that point, somewhere in our first six months together, I had gone from 'snack lady' to 'Mom.' That moment taught me that teaching joy meant holding space for shame and encouraging vulnerability. I had to demonstrate that even if the world judged them, they could learn to celebrate themselves anyway.

At the grocery store, when Gio did something silly with a box of cereal, I whispered to Judy, "Notice how Gio laughed? Remember that sound. Try it when you feel ready." And, slowly, between cartoon nights and tickles and silly faces, her unique version of laughter began to evolve. Her laugh had its pitch lowered, rhythm loosened, and warmth leaked in.

Teaching her to smile and laugh was a chapter in Judy's healing, but joy stretched beyond facial muscles. It meant nurturing the experiences that make childhood bright: running barefoot across the lawn, catching fireflies at dusk, painting her nails every rainbow color imaginable, chasing kites in an autumn breeze.

It meant orchestrating surprise dance parties in the living room and building pillow forts so grand that they became secret castles. It meant reading "Green Eggs and Ham" with a silly voice until we all collapsed into giggles: her, the other kids, even me.

Each time Judy threw her head back and laughed, real laughter that was free of fear, my heart soared. One afternoon, as she twirled in a sunbeam streaming through the window, she let out a laugh so genuine that it echoed down the hallway. I froze, listening, and tears blurred my vision. In that laugh, I heard the child she was always meant to become: unfettered, fully alive, delighting in the simple things. A child who knew how to laugh.

Who trains adoptive parents for this? Who tells them that their children might not instinctively know how to be happy, how to smile, or how to laugh and that you will literally have to teach them what joy looks like? The truth is, there is no manual for this. There's only the daily choice to show up, to practice patience, to celebrate tiny wins and rush to catch falls.

For Judy, and for all of us in that home, learning joy was a collaboration. It required my presence. It was me holding her, guiding her, and demonstrating over and over that laughter is safe. It demanded her courage to risk making a "wrong" sound, to cringe at stares, and then to persist until a genuine smile found its way onto her face. It took Gio joining in, modeling the behavior, showing that laughter could be a shared expression.

Joy was never a destination. It was a skill learned one moment at a time, in mirrors and tickles, in bursts of sunshine and bedtime lullabies. Judy's transformation from constrained smiles to laughter that filled a room is one of the most beautiful stories I've lived. And though shadows of her past still linger, every day she chooses joy, she reaffirms that her past does not define her.

In teaching her how to laugh, I learned anew what it means to be vulnerable, to guide another into fullness of life, and to celebrate the small steps that lead to healing. For any adoptive parent wondering if it's worth the effort, I say this: joy, once learned, becomes a fortress. It shelters a soul from despair. And for children like Judy, a single genuine laugh can shine a light so bright it banishes the darkest memories just long enough to remind them, and all of us, that life can still be beautiful.

Lessons in the Wilderness

The wilderness is a place of waiting, learning, and growth. For children like Judy, joy wasn't something that came naturally; it had to be learned. Just like the Israelites in the wilderness, who longed for the Promised Land, sometimes joy feels distant, unfamiliar, even impossible.

Yet God calls us to choose joy even in the desert:

"Rejoice in the Lord always. I will say it again: Rejoice!" (Philippians 4:4)

Joy is a seed planted in barren soil. I often told my children, "Joy is a choice. Choose joy." Teaching laughter and smiles was part of guiding them through the wilderness of their past hurts toward healing.

I often had to take my own advice. When I felt like I was drowning in the weight of adoption struggles I had to choose not to focus on my failed expectations but instead cling to every glimmers of hope. I had to set my mind on things above.

In those dry, lonely seasons, the Lord promises:

"The Lord is close to the brokenhearted and saves those who are crushed in spirit" (Psalm 34:18).

Like water in the desert, God's presence refreshes weary hearts. Each small smile or laugh is a step closer to the promised joy waiting beyond the wilderness.

So, if you find yourself wandering through your own wilderness, hold on to this truth: joy can grow here too, when you choose it daily and trust God's timing.

"You will go out in joy and be led forth in peace" (Isaiah 55:12).

Even in the wilderness, joy is possible. Choose it.

Prayer:

> *Lord, in the dryness of the wilderness, teach me to choose joy even when it feels impossible. Help me to see the small moments of hope and laughter as signs of Your healing and presence. Refresh my weary heart with Your love and remind me that joy is not just a feeling, but a choice rooted in You. Lead me forward with peace, and let Your joy be my strength each day. In Jesus' name, Amen.*

11

For eight years, survival was my life.

Cleaning up after a teenager wasn't unusual, but this wasn't typical. It wasn't medical. It wasn't developmental. It was psychological. Manny would soil himself intentionally and walk around unfazed, as if daring me to break.

And I did. Often.

I tried to hide how deeply it affected me. I told myself to stay calm. But he had found the one thing that pierced straight through all my defenses. I cried. I pleaded. I shouted. And he watched, with blank detachment or worse, quiet satisfaction. That was the point. This wasn't about the mess; it was about control.

He knew this behavior cut me deeper than anything else. With other challenges, I could sometimes mask my emotions. But this? This made me feel small, helpless, and ashamed. And every time I reacted emotionally, it reinforced something in him. A smirk. A shrug. A silent message: I own this moment. And sometimes I feared he was right.

He had full access to a bathroom. Nothing was stopping him. Yet he chose to go on the floor in his room, deliberately. Repeatedly. My sister once suggested I lay down plastic to protect the carpet. I was desperate enough to try.

I placed a large plastic tarp that covered every square inch of carpet in his room.

The next morning, I found the plastic carefully ripped in a circular hole - just big enough for him to put his private into the hole granting him access to the carpet beneath the tarp. He had peed directly onto the carpet through the opening. That's when I stopped pretending. No part of this was confusion or carelessness. It was deliberate. It was sabotage. He wanted to deface the things that were mine: my home, my energy, my hope. And every time, it worked.

So we tried a new strategy. I started walking him to the bathroom and waiting nearby. I thought maybe the structure would help. Maybe my proximity. But afterward, I'd step into disaster: waste on the floor, in the sink, in the tub. Hand towels used instead of toilet paper. Mats ruined. Not just a mess, It was warfare, played out in waste from a teenager.

Doctors ruled out any medical issue. Therapists agreed, this was about power. It wasn't simply defiance. It felt like domination. A twisted attempt to assert control by breaking me in the most degrading way possible.

And it didn't stop in the bathroom.

He couldn't be trusted even for a minute. Once, while waiting for the schoolbus, he knocked his sister down and beat her with a stick. Another time, he hurled rocks at his brother without warning. Even the school bus, crowded with peers, didn't stop him from whispering disturbing things to his sister in a chilling sing-song voice.

I brought everything to the therapists, hoping, begging, for help. But the response was always the same: Document it. Don't leave him alone with the others. Manny how do you feel about what you did? No plan. No support. Just a warning and a clipboard.

At school, it was worse. Manny wore a perfect mask. Teachers saw a quiet, quirky child. They didn't witness the chaos, the manipulation, the darkness we lived with daily. When I tried to explain, I could see it in their eyes: they didn't believe me. Or worse, they thought I was the problem.

* * *

And yet, I knew. I felt it in my bones. He was dangerous. I didn't have proof, he was too careful for that, but my gut screamed. I couldn't always explain why. But the fear was real.

I remember the day I had a newborn baby. Manny came home from school early, before I'd had a chance to use the bathroom. I hesitated. Could I leave the baby, just for a moment?

I placed the baby in the bassinet just outside the bathroom door, told Manny to sit on the stairs, and rushed in. The entire time I prayed, God, please protect my baby.

When I came out, he was quietly creeping toward the bassinet. I got there in time. Nothing happened. But the image of him silent, calculated, and closing in shook me to my core.

That was life back then: a low, constant hum of dread. He was getting older, stronger, and more adept at hiding his intentions. The threat was no longer abstract; it was real, present, and unpredictable. I lived on high alert, always scanning, always bracing. I managed to keep the other children safe from him, but the cost was my own unraveling. My nerves were threadbare, worn down by the weight of constant vigilance.

One night, not long after the baby was born, I woke suddenly. Something had shifted. The air felt off.

I opened my eyes and he was there. Standing at the foot of my bed. Silent. Still. Holding a knife.

The only light came from the moon, just enough to see the glint of the blade. His eyes weren't on the baby. They were fixed on me.

He didn't move. He didn't speak. He just stood.

In an instant, my mind raced through what felt like a thousand questions, though only a few truly mattered:

How long had he been standing there, watching me sleep?

* * *

Why was he holding a knife?

Sleep vanished, replaced in a heartbeat by a surge of adrenaline. I rose to my feet, flipped on a light and deliberately made myself appear larger, stronger, knowing I was alone that night. My husband wasn't home.

Of course Manny would choose this moment. Of course he'd wait until I was unprotected to try something.

My voice was steady, even though my heart pounded.

"Manny, give me the knife and go to bed."

For a second, he hesitated; flickers of indecision crossing his face. He wasn't the kind to lash out in the open. Manny was covert, calculated. He preferred shadows and secrecy. But now that I was awake, he'd lost that edge. Whatever he'd planned, it wasn't meant to happen in the light.

After a long pause, he dropped the knife on the floor, not in my hand, and turned without a word. He walked back to his room like nothing had happened.

But something had. And I wouldn't forget it. All my doubts disappeared. The fear I'd lived with had taken form. It stood at the end of my bed, inches from where I slept.

When we adopted Manny, I believed we were giving a child hope and healing. I never imagined I'd be bringing danger into our home. But I couldn't send him back. Social workers warned if we tried to give him back they would take our other children as well and charge us with child abandonment with Manny.

I was trapped. With him. With the fear. With the weight of a decision I couldn't undo.

After that night, we installed alarms on every bedroom door. Now, any movement in or out of a room triggered a loud chime. We weren't a family; we were a house under siege.

We locked up every knife. Stopped using silverware at the table. Plastic only. Kitchen knives were kept in a safe. Used, cleaned, locked away. It was the only way to sleep at all.

Our home had transformed. Once joyful, faith-filled, and open, it now felt like a fortress. One child's presence had turned us all into guards and prisoners. The other children in my home had lost the peaceful home they should have grown up in because of Manny. That is a pain I will carry with me always.

I had set out to rescue, but instead, I was being pulled under. And no one told me a child could have that kind of power.

And yet, even in the darkness, there were glimpses of light.

I remember visiting my mom without Manny once, and one of my children smiled. Really smiled. And I realized; I hadn't seen that in months.

That's when it hit me. We were ALL drowning.

I made a vow: I wouldn't let the dysfunction steal their light.

I couldn't change what we were living through. But I could fight to preserve joy. Manny went to bed by eight each night. That became sacred time. It was an hour to play games, read, and laugh. We began homeschooling the others, while Manny stayed in public school. It gave us precious, peaceful hours each day.

They were small things. But they reminded us who we were before this storm.

And that became my mission: to fight for the children who could still be saved.

No matter what Manny brought into our lives, the path became clear. I had to rebuild a safe, loving home for the ones still reaching for the light.

Lessons in the Wilderness

The wilderness is not just a place of trial, but a sacred space where God refines us teaching patience, shaping our character, and calling us to trust Him more deeply. Like the Israelites who wandered for decades, we learn that this journey is not about what we see or feel, but about walking by faith in God's promises.

Yet, the Israelites also teach us a sobering lesson: when the waiting grows long and the pain presses in, it's tempting to fix our eyes on the source of our suffering: the person who hurts us, the fear that haunts us, the chaos that surrounds us. In their weariness, the Israelites created idols, forgetting the true God who had delivered them from Egypt.

We must not fall into the same trap.

In our wilderness, instead of focusing on the difficulties that feel unbearable, God calls us to lift our eyes to Him. To seek His face, not our circumstances. To listen for His voice, not the noise of pain and fear.

"The Lord is good to those whose hope is in him, to the one who seeks him; it is good to wait quietly for the salvation of the Lord." (Lamentations 3:25-26)

This waiting is active, not passive. It's a quiet surrender that says, "God, You are greater than my fear. Your timing is perfect. Your love never fails."

You may feel trapped, like the storm will never end. I'm here to say it does eventually end and God's faithfulness is greater than the darkest night. He is molding your heart in this desert, preparing you for the promised land of peace.

Though the battle feels endless continue to fight to protect what is good.

Hold fast, weary warrior.

* * *

God sees every tear.

He hears every prayer.

And He will lead you out of the wilderness in His perfect time.

"Wait for the Lord; be strong and take heart and wait for the Lord." (Psalm 27:14)

Prayer:
> *Father God, in the midst of this wilderness, help me to fix my eyes on You, not on my struggles. When fear and pain threaten to overwhelm, remind me to seek Your face and trust Your perfect timing. Strengthen my heart to wait quietly and patiently, knowing Your love never fails. Help me to resist the temptation to look to false idols or quick fixes. Carry me through this season, and lead me into the peace You have promised. Thank You for seeing my tears and hearing my prayers. In Jesus' name, Amen.*

12

I remember when Gio first came to us, we mentioned something about God and he looked up at us with honest confusion and asked, "Who's that?" He didn't even know who God was, let alone Jesus. In so many ways, it felt like starting completely from scratch. We were teaching the basics of faith, trust, love, even how to use the bathroom. Instead of those firsts being with a newborn, we were starting with a five-year-old who had already survived a lifetime of chaos.

Every lie he told and every line he crossed I had to ask: Is this sin or survival? And more often than not, the answer was simply, 'Both. So love him through it anyway.'

One of Gio's biggest struggles was his deep fear of getting in trouble. That fear led to lying and sneaking becoming almost second nature for him, and those were the hardest habits to break. He also had a bond with Manny, even though I spent so much time shielding him from Manny's harm. That trauma bond between them was unhealthy, but powerful; it kept Gio tethered to patterns and mindsets he desperately needed to escape.

Manny hated us, and he wanted Gio to hate us too. I always knew when Manny had time to whisper his bitterness into Gio's ears: like on the school bus, when no one was watching. Gio would come home with his shoulders hunched, his gaze distant. The bright, affectionate little boy would suddenly go cold, angry, and withdrawn. It was like we had to win him back every single time. And we did, again and again.

* * *

He didn't come to us knowing how to live. But he came ready to survive. And somewhere between the empty candy wrappers, the poop in the vents, and the lies he began to learn what love looked like, even when it told him no.

Some days it felt like all we accomplished was undoing. Undoing years of confusion. Undoing lies someone else had whispered into his soul. Undoing the instinct to hide, to hoard, to hurt himself before anyone else could. And yet, beneath all of that, there was always something steady in Gio: a little boy who wanted to love and be loved, even if no one had shown him how yet.

He wanted, deep down, to be good. But he didn't yet know how to say no to himself. He had spent so much of his early life doing whatever it took to survive by sneaking, hiding, manipulating that those instincts had become automatic. He didn't lie because he was rebellious; he lied because he was scared. He didn't sneak because he wanted to defy us; he snuck because he wasn't sure he could live without the things he thought he needed.

Gio had always been clever. Thoughtful. Strategic.

So in his later teen years, when he decided to sneak something into the house, he didn't just stash it under his mattress or bury it in the bottom of a sock drawer. He removed the shoe molding from the base of the bathroom cabinet. Cut a hole just big enough to slide a phone into. Then pressed the molding back into place so seamlessly, we never suspected a thing.

He was calm those months. Steady. Even lighthearted.

We had no idea.

And then came Sunday.

We were all sitting in church when the pastor began preaching a message called Burn the Ships. He spoke about temptation: not just resisting it, but removing the path back to it. "Don't just say no," he said. "Cut off the return route. Burn the bridge. Burn the boat. Burn the back door."

Gio didn't say a word afterward. Didn't mention it in the car. Ate lunch like normal. Went about the rest of the day as if it hadn't unsettled anything inside him.

Then, that night, he sent us a message.

I opened it on my phone and hit play. The video was simple. It was just Gio, sitting out near the barn, face serious but steady.

"I need to confess something," he said. "I've been hiding a secret phone in the house. You didn't know, and I didn't want you to know. But this morning at church, that message… it got to me. The part about burning the ships. I realized I'd left myself a way back to the things I said I wanted to walk away from."

He looked down for a moment, then back at the camera.

"I already took care of it."

The next clip started automatically.

It was shot shaky, handheld, like he'd propped his phone against something nearby. It was the hidden phone, the one he'd smuggled in and kept secret for months. The one where he could text friends and girls we had told him were no good. The one where we didn't have life360 tracking was sitting on a rock out by the barn.

And then, on-screen, Gio lifted his BB gun.

No fanfare. No anger.

Just a series of quick shots crack, crack, crack and the phone was in pieces. Shattered glass, fragments scattering into the dirt.

The video ended.

He hadn't done it for attention. He didn't even ask for a response. Just quietly chose to cut off the escape route, to make it impossible to go back.

There was no punishment. We didn't need one.

Conviction had done what control never could.

Out there by the barn, in a quiet act of repentance, our son destroyed what had once held power over him, not because we told him to...

But because, for the first time, he wanted to be free.

That wasn't the last time Gio would sneak. His old habits weren't broken overnight. But that moment marked something new in him, a shift. A flicker of internal war, where he was no longer just hiding things from us. He had started to feel the weight of hiding from himself. From God.

His follow-through wasn't always perfect, but the desire was real. Even in his mess-ups, there was this unmistakable ache in him to do right. Not just to please us, but because he was beginning to care about what kind of person he was becoming.

God had not forgotten this child. And though Gio didn't yet know who God was, he was already being pursued. Sometimes, healing doesn't begin with a miracle. Sometimes, it begins with a snack bowl on the table and the promise that no matter how many times we had to win him back... we would.

Lessons in the Wilderness

Transformation rarely happens all at once. Often, it unfolds quietly step by step, day by day beneath the surface where we cannot always see it.

With Gio, I didn't know he was being changed. Some days, his behaviors felt so deeply woven into his brokenness that I feared we might lose him completely. I worried that the damage was too great, the darkness too thick. But through it all, I held tightly to God's Word. Sometimes I failed at this, but I always tried to follow the call to love him without compromise, to extend grace and forgiveness, and to teach truth even when it was hard.

The seeds of faith, planted in the soil of his wounded heart, were growing, though I couldn't see it. The quiet work of the Spirit was happening behind the scenes. It wasn't until Gio stepped into adulthood and left our home that I finally glimpsed the transformation God had been shaping all along.

This journey taught me what it truly means to walk by faith and not by sight, to obey God's commands without immediate proof that our efforts are bearing fruit.

"Now faith is confidence in what we hope for and assurance about what we do not see" (Hebrews 11:1).

If you feel weary, if the progress feels invisible or the waiting endless, remember: God's work is often silent. It may look like small moments of teaching, patient conversations, repeated corrections, or simply choosing to love day after day.

These are the steps of grace in motion.

Hold on to hope. Keep planting truth and love. Trust that God is at work, even when you cannot see it yet.

"He who began a good work in you will carry it on to completion until the day of Christ Jesus" (Philippians 1:6).

Your faithfulness matters. Your prayers are not wasted. The transformation you long to see is happening. Sometimes slowly, sometimes quietly, but always surely.

Prayer:
Lord, in moments when change feels invisible and hope grows faint, remind me that You are always at work—even when I cannot see it. Give me the courage to keep loving, teaching, and trusting Your timing. Help me to rest in Your promise that You will finish what You have started. Strengthen my faith to persevere, knowing transformation happens one small step at a time. Amen.

* * *

In the years after trauma, the heart often beats to rhythms we cannot predict. For Judy, those first five years under our roof were marked by emotional storms: sudden outbursts and waves of panic that no one could have anticipated.

Her grief and fear often surfaced as rage. With Judy, we learned that healing is rarely linear: even in her bravest moments, old survival instincts lingered just beneath the surface. Her recovery demanded not just gentleness, but relentless persistence.

From the beginning, Judy had no tools to manage her emotions. The smallest frustration like a broken crayon, a spilled cup, even a slightly raised voice could trigger a full collapse. One moment she'd be quietly playing, the next overwhelmed by tears, shouting, or thrashing.

Judy didn't just melt down; she exploded.

There was no confusion in those moments. No quiet trembling or tears. Just rage. Pure, hot, unfiltered rage, like her tiny body had become a conduit for something much bigger than her. Her eyes would harden, her jaw would clench, and she would lash out by kicking, slapping, and scratching anything to let the fire inside her out.

She didn't mean to hurt people. But in those moments, she didn't care if she did.

One therapist suggested we start with the basics. An emotion chart. We hung it on the fridge at her eye level: rows of cartoon faces with labels like angry, sad, scared, guilty, excited. When she was regulated, she could point to the one she was feeling and we'd help her cope through play, movement, or calming activities. But when she wasn't regulated? When the storm took over?

The chart might as well have been blank.

One afternoon, the rage came fast. I don't even remember what set her off. Maybe it was something small: a toy she couldn't find, or a request she didn't want to follow. But her response wasn't small.

* * *

She screamed, fists clenched, body shaking. Her face flushed deep red as she charged across the hallway, knocking things over as she went. I stepped in quickly and wrapped my arms around her: not to punish, not to restrain, but to anchor. To keep her from hurting herself. Or me. Or anyone else.

She thrashed in my grip, clawing at my skin, shouting words that didn't even make sense. Her body was wired for war, and I was the closest thing to fight.

"Let me go!" she shrieked.

"I'm here," I said, keeping my voice low and even. "I'm not letting you hurt yourself. You're safe, Judy."

She didn't want safety. Not then. She wanted destruction.

And that's when it happened.

One of the toddlers, hearing the commotion, wandered too close. Chubby hands holding a sippy cup, soft eyes blinking at the chaos.

"Mommy?" they asked, unsure.

"Stay back!" I called out, but the words were too late.

Judy, still raging, escaped from my arms, turned, and slammed the nearest door with all the strength her six-year-old frame could manage.

It connected with a sickening thud.

The toddler collapsed with a scream: piercing, high, and sharp enough to slice right through the moment. I released Judy and scooped them into my arms, already panicking. Their little face was contorted in pain, tears streaking their cheeks, one arm dangling motionless at their side.

"I'm so sorry, I'm so sorry, let me see," I whispered, trying not to let my voice shake.

* * *

They couldn't move it.

I feared the worst, a break. We rushed to urgent care. Miraculously, it wasn't broken. But the muscle and tissue damage was bad enough that they couldn't use that arm for nearly two weeks.

Back home, before we had left for urgent care, Judy didn't seem to care.

Not at first.

She paced the hallway, still fuming. Still defiant. Her face hard with the aftershock of rage. I wanted to believe she hadn't meant it, but in that moment, she looked like she meant all of it.

Only hours later, after she had finally calmed, her breathing slowed, and her body began to soften, did she seem to register what she had done.

"Did I hurt them?" she asked in a whisper, voice barely audible.

I nodded. "Yes."

Her eyes filled with tears. "I didn't mean to."

"I know," I said, exhausted. "But that doesn't undo the hurt."

She crumbled. Quiet this time. Ashamed. She curled into my lap like a child half her size and cried until her cheeks were raw.

That night, after everyone was asleep, I stood at the fridge, staring at the chart.

Angry. Sad. Scared. Guilty.

Judy had felt all of them.

But none of those faces could ever fully capture what it meant to be a child filled with rage they couldn't explain, hurting the people they loved most and hating themselves for it afterward.

* * *

So I stayed.

I stayed through the rage.

Through the storm.

And through the remorse that always came after.

Because Judy didn't just need help identifying her emotions.

She needed to believe she wasn't beyond love, even when her worst self came out.

Everything began to shift. It changed slowly, and almost imperceptibly when Judy was six, almost seven.

She'd been with us for a while by then. We had routines, structure, love, all the things she never had before. But trauma doesn't vanish overnight. Judy still carried the weight of it in her small frame, and most days, that meant a home filled with unpredictable explosions. Not just hers, but her older brothers were still struggling too, and their chaos bled into everything. Even in the moments when she was calm, they weren't. Their constant friction kept her nervous system on high alert.

And then that summer, for the first time, she got a break from it all.

She spent two months with my mom.

It wasn't a break from love. We'd given her that every day. But it was a break from the noise. From the volatility. From the undercurrent of survival energy that filled our home because of her brothers' histories.

At Grandma's, Judy found peace.

She still had the exact same rules and boundaries as she did in our home. Consistency was crucial. Structure and predictability that mirrored her home life with us were the foundation of her healing. But everything moved slower. Gentler. More predictable. My mom's days had a quiet rhythm: breakfast at the table, long walks through the neighborhood, puzzles in the afternoon sun. And Judy, freed from the need to brace for someone else's outburst, began to relax.

"She's so soft here," my mom told me over the phone. "Like she's finally exhaling."

That softness wasn't just about peace; it was about attention too.

One day, Grandma and my sister took her shopping for clothes. Not because she'd outgrown what she had, just because they wanted her to feel special. They let her pick out sparkly tops, soft leggings, even a new hoodie with a unicorn on it.

"She held everything like it was made of diamonds," my sister later told me. "She kept saying, 'For me? All this is for me?'"

And it was.

Not because she'd earned it.

Not to manage a meltdown.

Just because she was loved.

She came back to grandmas glowing, I heard.

It wasn't that she'd never been shown love before. We had poured love into her day and night, but this was the first time she'd had space to absorb it without the emotional noise of survival in the background. At Grandma's, she saw what normal looked like. What safe looked like when it wasn't constantly battling chaos.

One night, not long after she came home, I found her brushing her hair slowly in front of the mirror.

"I'm doing it like Grandma showed me," she said with a quiet grin. "Slow and gentle. So it doesn't hurt."

Then she smiled at her reflection, truly smiled.

* * *

That summer didn't change who she was. It revealed what was already inside her: the girl who wanted peace. Who could receive love without flinching. Who knew how to be gentle when the world around her finally felt gentle, too.

It wasn't just Grandma.

It was the quiet.

It was the stillness.

It was a season of rest from the chaos that had taught her to survive.

And in that season… she began to heal.

When Judy returned in the fall, I saw the change: fewer tantrums, a softer gaze, a quiet willingness to try. Instead of lashing out when frustrated, she might retreat to a corner and rock herself gently until calm returned. It wasn't perfect, but it was progress.

Even as Judy grew, some instincts clung to her. Nighttime remained difficult. Despite calmer days, she often crept into the pantry in the middle of the night, eating fistfuls of marshmallows as if tomorrow's meals might disappear. I'd hear the crinkle of wrappers and gently guide her back to bed, reassuring her that food would always be there. But her fear of scarcity was not so easily quieted.

Judy also struggled with honesty. Small lies, about chores or cookie jars, were common. We came to understand these weren't acts of rebellion, but shields. Telling the truth felt dangerous to a child shaped by punishment and fear. She hadn't learned that safety could live on the other side of confession.

One of the most complex dynamics was Judy's bond with her biological brother, Gio. I had hoped their shared history would be a source of comfort. Instead, it became a fortress. Together, they closed ranks: speaking in whispers, keeping the rest of us at arm's length.

I overheard them once behind a closed bedroom door: two voices low and serious, layered with something heavier than simple frustration.

"They'll never get it," Judy muttered.

"They don't know what it's like to be us," Gio replied.

Their words stung. But they made a heartbreaking kind of sense.

They weren't just close, they were bonded in survival. Their connection wasn't built on shared hobbies or laughter. It was built on fear and a connection of shared biology. On all the things they'd endured side by side before ever coming into our home. Letting someone else in, especially a new parent, a new sibling, felt like betrayal.

And that bond? It wasn't always tender. Sometimes it turned sharp. Defiant. Protective in the wrong ways.

If we corrected one of them, the other bristled. Eyes narrowed. Walls went up.

"We're blood," they'd mutter under their breath. "They're not even our real parents."

It wasn't just anger, it was loyalty forged in trauma. And that loyalty came at a cost.

Sometimes their fear of being replaced or overlooked spilled onto the other kids. Even the smallest conflict could spiral fast. I remember once catching wind of a conversation they'd had about one of their younger siblings: someone they saw as "the favorite." Their words had taken a dark, morbid turn. They were joking, they claimed, but the language they used… no child, no anyone, should speak that way about their sibling.

It shook me.

Not because I thought they meant it literally, but because I realized how numb they were to the impact of those words. To them, it was just another coping mechanism. Another way to take control of something they didn't understand: love that wasn't earned through pain.

We knew we couldn't force our way through that wall. There was no shortcut to healing.

And slowly, inch by inch, Judy's posture toward her non-biological siblings shifted. The walls between them didn't disappear, but they started to thin.

One night, as we sat talking on her bed late into the night, she asked, "It's okay to love Gio and still like the others too, right?"

I smiled. "Absolutely. Love doesn't run out. You don't have to choose."

She didn't say anything after that. Just nodded and pulled the blanket up to her chin.

Her early years taught us that trauma isn't tucked neatly in the past. It spills forward. It demands attention. Her outbursts, her food hoarding, her lies, they were all rooted in a brain trying to survive.

Her bond with Gio showed us that even the deepest love can become a shield. It also revealed that trust can grow, even from behind high walls.

Healing isn't a straight line. Sometimes it races forward, sometimes it falters. Judy's journey showed us the value of staying steady: holding her when she was at her worst, speaking gently when the truth felt dangerous, and celebrating the smallest step toward openness.

Most of all, "weathering the storm within" meant learning that love doesn't crash its way in. It knocks softly. It waits patiently. It shows up again and again. And slowly, in the wake of each storm, calm can return.

Judy's growing ability to regulate her emotions, to share space and affection, to trust and be trusted. These became our victories. In the quiet afterward of a peaceful bedtime or a shared smile we saw the proof: even the fiercest internal storms can yield to calm skies.

Lessons in the Wilderness

With all the challenges of raising my adoption children, especially Judy, I often felt weak and like a failure. There were times I thought I had let her down, like when I sent her to my mom's for the summer, wondering if I was giving up. But through it all, I learned this truth: God doesn't need our perfection. He only asks for our willing "yes."

Each morning, no matter how many times I stumbled or failed the day before, I chose to say yes again. Yes to patience. Yes to love. Yes to starting over. And every time I said yes, God met me there. He took my small, imperfect yes and transformed it into something beautiful.

God's strength shines brightest in our weakness, and all He wants is our willingness to try.

You don't have to have it all figured out. You don't have to have succeeded yesterday or even the whole of last year. Just say yes. Say yes to showing up again today. Say yes to trusting Him with the hard work of healing.

When you say yes, even in the middle of the wilderness, God will meet you there. He will take your yes and turn it into something greater than you could imagine like He did with my Judy.

So today, no matter what happened before, say yes. Say yes to grace. Say yes to hope. Say yes to the next step.

God is waiting at the door of your heart, ready to meet you at your yes.

"My grace is sufficient for you, for my power is made perfect in weakness." — *2 Corinthians 12:9*

Prayer:

Lord, when I feel weak and overwhelmed, remind me that You don't need my perfection, just my willing heart. Help me to say yes again today, to grace, to hope, and to the next step. Meet me in my weakness and transform my small yes into something beautiful. Your power is made perfect in my frailty. Amen.

13

Consumed with protecting the family from Manny, I missed something that now feels unforgivable: my other children's pain. They were struggling too, quietly and deeply, while I was stuck in survival mode.

The chaos Manny created took everything from me: my energy, my presence, even my ability to notice when someone else needed me. I wasn't the mother I wanted to be. I wasn't the mother they needed. Not because I didn't love them, but because I was constantly bracing for the next emergency.

That may be my greatest regret. Manny didn't just pull me down. He pulled all of us down. I lost myself. I became withdrawn, exhausted, depressed. Impatient. Isolated. And the ripple effects didn't stop with me.

The damage Manny caused, whether through his actions or the toll his behaviors took on our home, left a mark on every child in our family. The trauma wasn't his alone. We all lived it. We're all still healing from it.

Eventually, we made a decision that felt like our last lifeline: we moved closer to family. We had been living a thousand miles away, isolated and overwhelmed. Managing Manny's behaviors without support was slowly breaking me. So we packed up and moved to the same street as my mother.

My mom was the only one who truly saw what was happening. She didn't downplay it. She didn't blame me. She believed me. Completely. Manny's charm and well-practiced mask never fooled her. She saw through him from the beginning, and her presence became an anchor in the storm.

And for a while, things did get better. The alarms were still on the doors. The knives were still locked away. The children and animals still needed to be protected. But the intensity of Manny's behaviors' seemed to ease a little. Maybe it was the change of environment. Maybe it was the presence of someone who understood. For the first time in years, it felt like we could breathe again. But looking back, I hadn't learned to breathe; I had only learned to hold my breath longer.

Living near my mom gave me just enough support to begin seeing clearly again. I had already built some safeguards into our lives: Manny went to public school while I homeschooled the others. He had an early bedtime so our evenings could feel more peaceful. There were slivers of normalcy woven into the day, and I clung to them like lifelines.

As things calmed, those slivers began to feel more like real life and less like exceptions. I became laser-focused on one thing: protecting the happiness of my other children. I wanted to make sure Manny's darkness didn't swallow their childhoods.

Every morning after the school bus pulled away, we'd take a deep breath and let the tension fall. That was our time to laugh, to learn, to be a family without fear. Evenings, after Manny went to bed, became sacred. We'd play games, tell stories, eat snacks. Just be together safe and free.

It didn't erase the trauma. But it reminded us that trauma wasn't the only thing in our home. Joy could still exist. My children deserved that. And giving it to them, even in pieces, became the fire that kept me going.

There were still moments, moments that would sound alarming to anyone else. But when you've lived under constant stress, your sense of normal becomes warped. Things that should have been red flags started to feel like progress.

* * *

One of those times that should have been a red flag that things weren't getting better was when we thought we were giving him a bit of freedom.

Just a couple hours. Just the library.

"Manny," I said that afternoon, handing him a few dollars for snacks at the vending machine, "we'll be back at four. Stay inside."

He nodded, empty backpack slung over one shoulder, too-cool smirk in place. "Got it."

At first, everything seemed fine.

But when we pulled back into the parking lot later that day, Manny wasn't waiting on the library steps.

I scanned the sidewalk. Nothing.

Then I spotted him.

Jogging, half out of breath, across the parking lot from Walmart, overflowing backpack bouncing against his back.

I stepped out of the car. "Where were you?"

He flashed a grin, a little too smooth. "Walmart. Just looking around."

I narrowed my eyes. "Wasn't your backpack empty when we dropped you off?"

"It's nothing," he said, brushing past me. "Just snacks from the vending machine. Nothing big."

But something felt off.

When we got home, I waited until the others were distracted and called him into the kitchen.

* * *

"Open it," I said, nodding to the backpack.

He hesitated.

"Manny."

He unzipped it.

Out tumbled a pile of items. There were snacks, batteries, DVD's, clothes, even some cheap earbuds. Definitely not the kind of haul bought with two dollars.

"What is all this?" I asked, keeping my voice even.

He shrugged, already spinning. "It wasn't me. This guy outside Walmart asked me to hold his stuff for a minute and then he took off."

I just stared at him. We both knew it wasn't true.

But in that moment, strangely, I felt a flicker of relief. At least it was just petty theft. At least he hadn't hurt anyone.

Yet.

That "yet" lived in the back of my mind like a shadow.

Because there were other moments.

Moments like the one just a few weeks later. It started with something small; I can't even remember what. A boundary, probably. A rule he didn't like. I stood firm, expecting the usual pushback.

But then his face changed.

His eyes darkened. His whole body went rigid.

And in a blink, he lunged.

There was no warning. No buildup.

* * *

Just a flash of rage and his body crashing toward mine.

My breath caught in my throat.

But then, my husband stepped in. He had seen it from across the room, and in seconds he was between us, calm but firm, grounding the moment.

Manny froze, then backed off. Just like that, it was over.

But for me, it wasn't.

Not really.

Because once you've seen that switch, once you've felt your child's rage rise so suddenly and so violently, you don't forget it. You carry it with you. In your chest. In your breath. In the way your body tenses without permission.

I was okay. I was unharmed. This time.

But only because my husband had been home.

And what haunted me wasn't that moment. It was the question it left behind:

What happens next time, if my husbands not home?

I was afraid of Manny.

Afraid of what he might do if the storm came again and no one else was there to stop it.

Those moments should have been breaking points. And yet, to us, they felt like signs we were holding the line. The theft hadn't escalated. The hit hadn't landed. We were surviving. Barely.

Even at thirteen and fourteen, we were still finding jars.

Not forgotten water bottles or snack wrappers, jars of waste, hidden in corners of Manny's room.

It should have horrified us.

But it didn't. Not anymore.

Not after everything we'd seen.

By then, it felt... manageable. Contained. Like progress because he was no longer sitting in it and smearing it on the walls.

And that was the most disturbing part: not the jars themselves, but how numb we'd become to them. How distorted our sense of "normal" had grown. A house full of trauma will recalibrate your instincts until even the grotesque feels oddly routine.

Then there was the day I stripped his bed for laundry and found something I didn't expect.

Tucked behind the dresser was women's dirty underwear.

The underwear didn't belong to anyone in our home and Manny wasn't the kind of boy who easily connected with others, especially girls. Social situations were hard for him and he often struggled to read cues, hold eye contact, or have a conversation.

It was unlikely that a girl had willingly given these to him. Still I pushed down the growing suspicion that he might have taken them without permission from unsuspecting neighbors laundry basket. I didn't want to believe it, but I couldn't ignore it either.

When I asked him, he shrugged. "I found them by the lake. Thought it was funny."

He was half-laughing, trying to play it off. Just another joke. Just trash some teens had left behind.

But it wasn't funny.

It wasn't just the underwear. It was the way he watched me when I picked them up. His expression was unreadable at first, then it curled into a smile that made my skin crawl. It wasn't shame, or fear, or confusion on his face. It was something else. Something darker.

It was like he was savoring a new kind of power. Not the power of getting away with something, but the power of watching me be forced to touch what I didn't want to touch. The power of making me uncomfortable.

It was almost predatory, and in that moment, I felt less like his caregiver and more like his prey. His smile chilled me more than the discovery itself.

Something in me recoiled.

My gut twisted.

But I buried it. Like I had so many times before.

I wanted so badly to believe he was getting better. That the therapy, the structure, the love: it was all working. That these moments were just... residue. Not red flags.

Because when you're living in survival mode, you start grading on a curve.

You start calling "better than before" good enough.

And then came the knife.

It was late. A regular Tuesday. Dishes in the sink. Chores rotating between the kids.

I'd forgotten we'd used knives that night. Forgotten to lock them up afterward: something we'd grown lax about, maybe because the months had been calm. Maybe because hope is a sneaky thing, and it can lull you into letting your guard down.

"Manny," I said, "can you help dry these?"

* * *

He grumbled but stepped up beside me.

Picked up a knife.

And in one smooth, casual movement, turned to his brother and pointed it at him.

"I could kill you right now," he said, smiling.

Smiling.

The room stopped.

No screaming. No shouting. Just that quiet smile. Knife in hand. The air thick with something primal.

My body moved before my brain.

I reached across the counter and pulled it from his grip in one clean motion.

"Hey…" he started.

"No," I snapped, the word cutting sharper than the knife ever could.

I stood between him and his brother, heart pounding.

He backed off.

And I wasn't ready for that.

Not yet.

It should have been a crisis.

And it was.

But I didn't treat it like one.

I dried the rest of the knives myself. Sent the kids to bed. Told my husband quietly, later that night.

And I told myself it was a slip.

Not a spiral.

Because if I didn't minimize it, I would have to face it.

And what choices did I have?

The state had made the stakes painfully clear: if we disrupted the adoption and if we tried to step away, we risked jail time for "abandonment." Worse, we could lose custody of the other kids in our home.

That wasn't an option. So we stayed.

And told ourselves he was improving.

We convinced ourselves that it wasn't that serious. That it was a moment of poor judgment. That no one had been hurt. That he was learning. Growing.

Because sometimes, denial is the only oxygen you have left.

And when you feel trapped with no exit, even a lie that lets you sleep at night can start to feel like mercy.

We were so starved for hope that we mistook survival for healing. And for a while, I believed it. I let myself hope. I told myself maybe, just maybe, love and structure and time were helping.

But looking back now, I see the truth. Manny wasn't healing. He was just getting older. Not changed; just more careful. More subtle. Better at hiding. Even from me.

That realization broke something in me. I had started to let my guard down. Not completely, but a little. The alarms on doors were still there, but we weren't living like prisoners anymore. I believed things were safer.

* * *

One day, I stepped away. Just for a moment.

He was in the living room with the others. We were a big family. There were voices, movement, noise. I told myself there was safety in numbers. That someone would notice if something was wrong.

One of the younger kids had just been scolded by an older sibling over something small. Nothing major, just the usual sibling tension.

And that's when Manny saw his moment.

He softened his voice. Smiled. "Hey," he said to the younger one, "let's go play in the other room."

I was told later, It sounded innocent.

Kind, even.

I was tired. So tired.

Tired of being a warden instead of a mom. I wanted normal. I wanted to be able to fold a load of laundry in my room while my kids played quietly in the living room.

I was tired of the alarms and locked doors. Tired of the constant supervision. Tired of living under the weight of fear for the eight long years Manny had been in our home. I just wanted a breath. One breath where I didn't have to feel like a prison warden in my own home.

And in that breath, I convinced myself it was okay.

But it wasn't.

The truth didn't come from Manny.

It came later. Quietly. Hesitantly.

First from the child he'd tried to "go play" with. Then from Gio, who had walked into that room at just the right moment.

* * *

Manny had waited until they were alone.

He tried to harm the younger child, but he didn't succeed. Because Gio walked in.

And when Gio saw what was happening, Manny turned on him. Grabbed him by the neck and leaned in close.

"If you tell anyone," he whispered, "I'll kill you."

But the child had already gotten away. Manny hadn't counted on that. He hadn't gotten far enough to silence them. And he hadn't realized the one person brave enough to speak would be the one he'd just threatened.

Gio came to me. Trembling. Eyes wide. He told me everything.

And that was the moment I stopped pretending.

That was the moment the dam broke and the truth spilled out, not just about what happened in that room, but about what we'd been carrying for far too long.

Manny wasn't getting better.

He wasn't safe.

And it took a child's courage, a child he'd threatened, to make me face what I didn't want to admit.

That our home could no longer protect everyone.

And something had to change.

For eight years, the threats had always been aimed at me: spoken, snarled, or simmering just beneath the surface. I'd lived with the tension, the fear, the constant vigilance. But when it came to the other children, all I'd ever had were gut feelings. Warnings in my chest I couldn't prove.

* * *

Until now.

Now it wasn't just instinct. It was real. A child endangered. A threat made. A moment I hadn't stopped.

That was the moment everything changed. All the justifications, all the cautious hope, all the ways I'd tried to believe we were turning a corner, they collapsed under the weight of that one truth.

He wasn't just struggling. He was dangerous. And no amount of structure, love, or second chances could fix what he had done.

This wasn't progress. This was a predator learning to wait, to watch, to strike when no one was looking. That's when hope stopped being a lifeline and started becoming a liability. That's when hope became harm. The day I found out this story is the day Manny left our home never to return.

Lessons in the Wilderness: From Survival to Progress

In the wilderness of trauma and parenting, it's easy to mistake survival for progress. We tell ourselves that "better than before" is enough, even as warning signs grow louder. Our sense of normal adapts, and what should shock us begins to feel almost routine.

This reminds me of the Israelites' journey after God delivered them from Egypt. They witnessed miraculous signs: the Red Sea parting before their eyes, a pillar of fire guiding them by night, plagues that devastated Egypt while sparing God's people. Yet despite these undeniable acts of God's power, the Israelites often grew complacent. They forgot their role in God's plan: to obey, to trust, and to move forward.

What should have been a short journey to the Promised Land turned into forty years of wandering in the desert. They survived, but they did not progress. Fear, doubt, and disobedience held them captive in the wilderness longer than necessary.

Their story holds a mirror up to us. In our own wilderness seasons, whether raising traumatized children or healing from deep wounds, we can get stuck in survival mode, afraid or unsure how to step forward. But God calls us not just to endure, but to grow. To trust Him enough to obey, to keep moving, even when the path is uncertain.

Paul reminds us in Philippians 3:13-14:

"But one thing I do: Forgetting what is behind and straining toward what is ahead, I press on toward the goal to win the prize for which God has called me heavenward in Christ Jesus."

God's grace sustains us through the wilderness. His power is made perfect in our weakness (2 Corinthians 12:9). But He also invites us to partner with Him, to say yes to each new day, to each small step forward, trusting that He is working even when we cannot yet see the full picture.

Survival is necessary. It's a first step. But God desires the progress of transformation, healing, and growth. The wilderness is not just a place of waiting, but a place of preparation for all that He has planned next.

If you find yourself stuck in survival mode today, remember the Israelites' story. Don't settle for simply enduring. Listen for God's gentle call to obey, to trust, and to press forward, step by step, toward the abundant life He promises.

Say yes to the journey. Say yes to the work He's doing in you and your family, even when it's hard or slow. Survival is a season, not a destination; keep moving toward God's promises.

Prayer:

Father, in the wilderness seasons when survival feels like all I can manage, help me to hear Your call to move forward. Give me strength to press on, courage to trust Your plan, and faith to believe that You are working even when I can't see the way. Transform my endurance into growth and my waiting into preparation for the abundant life You have promised. Amen.

14

Gio was one of the quiet casualties of my war to protect him. So much of my energy was spent shielding him from Manny that I didn't realize how much help he still needed from me. I was so focused on defending him from obvious danger that I missed the quiet signals. The ones that didn't scream, but still meant something was breaking. He needed more of me, and I didn't see it until later.

When Gio walked in on Manny about to hurt one of our other children and after Manny threatened to kill him if he ever told, something in Gio changed. After Manny was finally removed from our home, a weight began to lift.

Gio started to breathe differently. Stand differently. Move differently. It was subtle at first, but unmistakable. Without the constant shadow of fear, he could finally begin figuring out who he really was. And for a while, things got better.

Gio had struggled to learn his whole life. His trauma had made even basic education feel like scaling a mountain. I'll never forget one of his kindergarten teachers bluntly telling me, "He's not going to get it. He'll just be graduated on." It broke my heart and it lit a fire in me. From that moment on, I poured in extra time, extra patience, extra belief. I refused to let that become his story.

And it didn't.

I don't want to get too far ahead of myself, but I will say this: that same boy, once written off in kindergarten, completed a two-year college degree before turning eighteen. He's living proof that early brokenness doesn't get the final word.

But Gio didn't start truly learning until Manny left. Until he finally felt safe, safe in our home and with me, his mind hadn't been free to open. Fear had made it impossible to absorb, to retain, to grow. But once that grip loosened, something remarkable began to happen. We would sit for hours on the couch together doing schoolwork, and for the first time, I could really reach him. He let me in.

That never would've happened while Manny was in the house. Gio wouldn't have dared sit close to me back then. Manny wouldn't have allowed it. His disapproval was loud, constant, and terrifying. Even if Manny wasn't saying anything, his presence in the room was enough to shut Gio down.

But once that oppressive presence was gone, Gio began to trust. He relaxed in small ways: leaning into conversations, lingering near me, laughing more freely. He began to grow in places that had been stunted for years.

And then, he began to open up.

I remember so many late-night talks with Gio: conversations where he would finally share his thoughts, his memories, his questions. After eight years in our home, it felt like we were just beginning to meet the real Gio. It was both beautiful and heartbreaking. Beautiful because he was blooming. Heartbreaking because of how long he'd been hidden.

I often wonder how much more healing could have happened if he'd had that safety earlier, if Manny hadn't cast such a long shadow. I don't live in that space, not for long. But the ache of that lost time still lingers. Some things can't be undone. We just move forward.

Another layer of complexity in Gio's story was that he was adopted alongside his biological siblings. In some ways, it was a gift. It preserved connection, history, familiarity. But it also made it harder for him to fully bond with us as his parents. There was always an unspoken sense that his loyalty belonged to his blood. No matter how much love we gave, we were never quite his mom and dad. Not fully. Not yet.

He'd spend hours talking and playing with Judy, but the moment we entered the room, he'd shut down or walk away. It wasn't overt disrespect, it felt more like a retreat. As if our presence disrupted something sacred to him, something fragile and tied to where he came from. It was like we were the reminder that things had changed, and not everyone wants change, even when it's safe.

Any time he faced a consequence, the walls would go up. He'd retreat behind that old defense: You're not my real parents. You don't have the right. It became his shield when things felt hard or unfair. That sentiment followed us through much of his childhood and adolescence: a painful reminder that his heart was still guarded, still unsure where it belonged.

But something shifted as Gio grew into adulthood. Slowly, quietly, he began to let us in, not just as caregivers or rule-makers, but as mom and dad. It didn't happen in one grand moment. There was no dramatic scene or teary confession. Just a steady opening over time: trust given in slivers, love returned in glances and small gestures.

It was the product of years of consistency, years of loving him even when he pulled away. Years of standing still while he ran in circles. Years of whispering the truth until he could finally hear it: You are safe. You are loved. You are ours.

And one day, as an adult when I'd given up on ever having him love us, he turned toward us fully. Not with words, but with presence. He lingered in conversations. He called just to check in. He asked for advice. He brought us into his world, not because he had to, but because he wanted to.

The boy who once kept secrets out of fear began sharing his life out of love. We didn't become his parents overnight. We became them one meal, one homework assignment, one hard conversation at a time.

The shift was so gradual we almost missed it, until one day, we didn't. One day, he called me "Mom," and it didn't sound borrowed. It sounded like it had always belonged to me. And in that quiet moment, I knew: we had made it through the wilderness together.

Lessons in the Wilderness

In the wilderness, it's easy to mistake silence for absence. When nothing seems to be changing, we wonder if our labor is in vain. But Jesus reminded us in the parable of the sower that seeds take root in different kinds of soil and the gardener's work often happens long before we see the first green shoot.

With Gio, there were years when I saw no visible change. The ground of his heart seemed hard. But the Master Gardener was tending it by softening the soil, pulling the weeds, and making it ready. There were moments when I let grief overtake me and I gave up.

I didn't stay in the place of being defeated in my relationship with him. I prayed and believed every time I saw anything that reminded me of his need. If I had given up entirely because nothing had sprouted, maybe the flower would never have bloomed.

The same is true for you. You may not see the progress. You may feel like nothing is taking root. But trust the One who sees below the surface. His hands are still working. His timing is still perfect. And the harvest He is growing will be worth the wait whether that harvest is in your own life or in the life of someone you are believing for a breakthrough.

"But the seed falling on good soil refers to someone who hears the word and understands it. This is the one who produces a crop, yielding a hundred, sixty or thirty times what was sown." —Matthew 13:23

Prayer:
Lord, help me to trust Your timing when I cannot see the growth beneath the surface. Give me patience and faith to keep planting, watering, and believing even in the silence. Soften my heart and the hearts I'm praying for, that Your harvest may come in Your perfect way and time.

Amen.

15

Judy's story took a decisive turn the summer she turned twelve. Up until then, she carried herself like someone always bracing for impact: eyes wary, smile measured, heart guarded. Years of fear and survival had shaped her. But something happened that summer. At a quiet church camp tucked in the hills, a spark of faith ignited in her and the weight she carried began to loosen.

She began to walk a new path, one shaped not by fear, but by grace. It didn't erase her struggles overnight, but created space for her to choose a new way of living: one rooted in love, family, and joy.

Judy experienced the most dramatic transformation of all and it can only be attributed to Jesus. When everything felt impossible, prayer was our only lifeline. One summer, as a teenager still carrying the echoes of her earliest years, she went to a church camp and returned radically changed. From that moment, everything shifted.

She didn't give many details at first, just said something about a worship night where she felt "known" in a way she hadn't before. But I noticed it immediately: the way she hugged her sisters instead of ignoring them, how she looked me in the eyes without flinching. Something had changed.

She came back from camp with a light in her eyes I had never before seen in her. Prior to camp, anger or despair had clouded her gaze; now, something gentle and determined shone through. She stopped participating in the unhealthy conversations with her brother, Gio, no longer retreating with him into whispered bitterness.

Instead, she reached out to us, making intentional efforts to connect. In family dinners, she offered to help set the table; when something upset someone in the family, she asked to talk it through rather than withdrawing.

Her choices changed, too. Instead of acting on old survival instincts like secretly hoarding snacks or fabricating elaborate lies, she began speaking truth. When she slipped up, she apologized without hesitation. It wasn't because she feared punishment, but because something in her heart had genuinely shifted. She was discovering the kind of brave vulnerability that faith can inspire: a willingness to risk being "seen" rather than hiding behind pain.

As Judy's faith deepened, she grew closer to our family. Mealtimes, which once felt tense, became opportunities for laughter and conversation. We started weekend rituals: late night talks in mom and dads room, shared chores, and family devotions. In those moments, Judy's laughter rose freely, no longer rehearsed or forced. She added her own voice to the family's joys, as though her heart had been unlocked.

But joy often comes at a price. As Judy drew nearer to us, her bond with Gio showed strain. It was as if he didn't know how to hold space for both his sister and her new faith. One day, Judy arrived home and found Gio waiting outside her room, arms crossed. Their usual greeting was gone.

For years, Gio had been her refuge. They'd whispered under blankets, shared inside jokes no one else understood, and survived the chaos side by side. That's why his words, "I don't know you anymore" landed like a slap.

Judy didn't cry right away. She nodded, quietly, and walked to her room. But behind closed doors, her world cracked open. How could the path that brought her peace take her away from the one person who'd always understood her?

Judy's face fell, heartbreak flickering in her eyes. For so long, their shared mantra had been: "We're blood. We only have each other." Now, by choosing Christ and embracing our family's love, she was inadvertently choosing to step outside that old comfort zone.

That decision to fully embrace her new way of living life was not immediate. Judy passed through a season of small compromises, caught between her desire to keep her brother close and the pull of her new faith. It wasn't just her personal convictions that made her and Gio have a wedge, it was her bond with us as her parents. Gone was the mantra of "we only have each other" and it was like Gio felt betrayed that she had allowed us into her heart.

At first when he would vent about us she would stay silent simply to keep peace. But each quiet compromise felt like a betrayal of what she knew was right.

One afternoon, sitting on her bed with the Bible open but untouched, Judy wept: "God, I want my brother back. But I also want You. I don't know how to have both." That prayer marked the turning point. Determined to remain faithful, Judy returned the next summer to church camp: this time with a resolve steeled by heartbreak.

In the early morning hush of that camp, when worship songs rose above the pine trees, Judy offered herself entirely. "Even if it costs me my brother, I choose You, Jesus." she whispered. When the sun broke through the canopy, it was as though her spirit broke free.

In the weeks after that second camp and a year after the first camp, both pain and healing unfolded. For a season, Gio distanced himself. He spent late nights in his room or left the house often. Judy's heart ached with each passing day that he stayed away: text messages unanswered, doors silent. Yet she clung to her faith, finding comfort in prayer and pouring her energy into connecting with the rest of us.

So she poured herself into the life she still had.

She trained with her dad for hours at her pole vaulting sport, pushing herself higher with each pole vault.

She helped her sisters with homework, took her little brother out for ice cream.

She joined the worship team. She led Bible studies. She started college early.

And through it all, she smiled, not the rehearsed smile of survival, but a new one. Unforced. Joyful. Whole.

One night, as we watched her laugh uncontrollably during a family game night, I found myself blinking back tears. This was our Judy, but lighter, freer, finally alive.

The more the pain of Gio's absence wounded her and continued the more she threw herself into living life to the fullest and loving each member of our family with all she had. She did everything to prove that family extended beyond a single bond of blood.

Bit by bit, Gio began to reappear in her life. The first sign was a text: "Can we talk?"

He invited her to a local coffee shop. "I missed you," Gio admitted, looking down at his coffee. "But I didn't know how to be close to you anymore. It felt like... you left me."

Judy reached across the table, her voice soft. "I didn't leave you, Gio. I just couldn't stay in the pain with you. I wanted more. For both of us."

He was quiet for a long time. Then, almost inaudibly, he said, "I was scared you wouldn't want me anymore. I still feel broken. It was easier to push you away than to risk being rejected by you."

She squeezed his hand. "I always will want you. I just had to learn how to love you without losing myself."

They spoke for hours about loyalty, about change, about what it means to truly support someone. When Gio finally reached across the table to hug her, it felt like two halves of a broken heart coming back together. Their bond wasn't the same as before; it was now built on a deeper respect and a new willingness to include everyone who loved them.

* * *

As Judy stepped into adulthood, she became more than a daughter. She became one of my very best friends. We shared our hopes and fears over late-night talks, sending each other prayer requests and verses from Scripture.

She amazed me constantly: enrolled in college courses while still in high school, earning top grades; serving on mission trips; and mastering the pole vault, winning many first-place medals.

Her faith extended into every corner of her life. When she fell short, perhaps responding too harshly to a sibling, she would quietly pray for forgiveness and then ask our forgiveness. I often watched her wipe away tears, whispering, "Mom, I'm so sorry. I messed up." And I would pull her into a hug and say, "You're not perfect and that's okay. We love you exactly as you are."

Yet beneath her confident glow, I could still see the echo of that fierce desire for perfection. Even in adulthood, when she sensed my disappointment over a missed commitment or a mistake, her face would pale as if the world had ended.

I'd remind her gently, "Sweetheart, our love isn't conditional. It doesn't shatter when you make a mistake." And slowly, year by year, those old fears loosened their hold.

Standing back now, I marvel at the fullness of Judy's joy. She is the first to arrive at church on Sunday mornings, worshiping with arms raised. She spends her evenings mentoring younger girls, helping them explore faith and healing. She still has moments of self-doubt, an occasional pang of "I must be perfect to be loved." But when that shadow crosses her eyes, she leans on the truth she's learned: grace is bigger than her mistakes.

I still am amazed at the moment she stood on the football field, facing a stadium full of her peers, unshaken and courageous ready to share her story with the world. She spoke openly about her traumatic past, but more than that, she spoke of the joy she's found in Jesus and how her past no longer defines her. With quiet strength, she turned her pain into purpose, using her story to offer hope to others who may be silently hurting.

* * *

When people meet Judy for the first time, they often say, "Her joy is contagious. How can she be that happy?" They don't know she was once trapped in fear and scarcity. They see only the light she now carries. And that is the miracle, how, in the hands of a loving God, Judy's brokenness was not only mended but transformed into radiant strength.

She is the beautiful part of adoption. With Manny, we offered a second chance but saw a life that couldn't be redeemed. With Gio, we saved a life and built a relationship that teetered between darkness and light and finally landed in light.

But with Judy, she taught us what true redemption looks like. We didn't simply rescue her; we witnessed a rebirth. She didn't just learn to cope; she learned to soar. She didn't merely find safety, she found joy.

When people meet Judy now, they often remark, "I've never met someone so joyful!"

They see her laughter, her service, her fierce love for others, but they don't see the shadows she walked through.

What they see is the miracle: a girl once bound by fear, now set free by grace.

And in every hug, every kind word, every radiant smile, she reminds us that redemption is real.

That healing is possible.

That joy, even for the most wounded hearts, is never out of reach

Remember that redemption is often costly. Healing a child scarred by trauma can feel impossible. But Judy's story reminds us: when faith meets persistence, the impossible becomes possible. She stands today not as proof of human strength alone, but as a living testimony to the grace that can turn ashes into beauty.

Lessons in the Wilderness

Judy's early years were like a desert. Fear and pain clung to her in ways that felt impossible to move. Some days, all I could see was dry ground stretching to the horizon. I prayed, I tried, I failed, I tried again. I didn't see much change, and part of me wondered if this was all there would ever be.

But God sees what I can't. He is the master gardener who works beneath the surface, and the water-bearer who brings life to the driest places.

In Judy's story, the "new thing" didn't rush in like a flood. It came in slow trickles — moments of trust, steps of obedience, little bursts of joy. Most of them I missed because I was still staring at the wasteland ahead.

Isaiah says, *"See, I am doing a new thing! Now it springs up; do you not perceive it? I am making a way in the wilderness and streams in the wasteland."* That's exactly what was happening, even when I couldn't see it. The wilderness wasn't wasted. It was the place where God's power and provision were most visible — where His stream ran sweetest.

Judy's redemption wasn't my doing. The only thing I did was keep showing up. Keep saying yes. Even on the days when my yes was reluctant, even when I felt like a failure, I gave Him the only thing I had — a willingness to try again. And God took that yes and made beauty grow where I thought nothing could live.

If you're standing in your own desert right now, don't give up. Water is moving underground. Life is coming. Say yes again today. Say yes tomorrow. Keep saying yes until the stream breaks through and turns your wasteland into a garden.

Prayer:

Father, in the dry and weary places, help me to trust Your unseen work. When I can't see change, remind me You are making a way and bringing streams in the wilderness. Give me the courage to keep saying yes, even when I'm tired or discouraged. Use my faithfulness to bring new life and beauty where I thought only emptiness remained. In Jesus' name, Amen.

16

That was it.

No more second chances.

I didn't care what CPS said, Manny would never set foot in our home again.

When he was eight or nine and I had to worry about him being unsafe with the other kids, it felt different. He was still just a child himself, only a few years removed from his own trauma. Part of me questioned whether he even fully understood how wrong his behavior was back then.

But now? At fourteen? He knew. He absolutely knew. And he chose to cross the line anyway.

There was no more room for doubt. No more mental gymnastics, trying to see things from his perspective. Our home had become a place of fear and silence for too long. And this time, the damage was minutes away from becoming irreversible if not for Gio's divine intervention.

Thank God for my mom. I didn't care anymore what the state threatened. If they wanted to take all our children because we refused to let Manny stay, so be it. I refused to be held captive to Manny's terror any longer due to the states threats. My mom, in her deep love and unwavering clarity, stepped in.

* * *

At seventy years old, she didn't hesitate. She walked into the fire so I could pull the others out.

She offered to take Manny in at fourteen years old and raise him for the final stretch until adulthood. She saw what I saw. She understood what it was costing us to keep him under our roof.

We were one of the lucky ones. I know many families who had a child like Manny, deeply troubled and unsafe to have in the home, but no one stepped in to help them. One mother I knew had a son who attempted to assault his younger sister.

Out of desperation, she placed him in a residential facility. But his behavior there was so disruptive that even the professionals couldn't manage him. When the facility expelled him, they demanded she come pick him up. She refused, asking the obvious question: If trained professionals couldn't keep him from harming others, how could she protect her daughter at home?

Instead of offering her help, the state threatened to remove all her other children if she didn't take her son back accusing her of child abandonment of the child with behavioral issues. It was the same threat I had received. Sadly, this kind of coercion is not rare. It's a common tactic used to pressure parents, no matter how valid their concerns.

Another mother faced something similar, but this account had to do with her adopted daughter. The girl repeatedly made false accusations against the family, triggering constant investigations. Each time, the claims were proven untrue, but the emotional toll on the family was devastating. Their children lived under a cloud of fear, worried they might be taken away at any moment, despite their parent's innocence.

I could share countless stories like these: families who fared far worse than we did. The common thread is this: when their child with reactive attachment disorder began to exhibit dangerous behaviors, they had no support system. No safety net. Unlike us, they didn't have someone willing to step in during their pivotal moment. And because of that, many of them were left to suffer alone.

* * *

Without my mother's offer, I honestly don't know what we would have done. Maybe my husband and I would have had to split our family: one of us living with Manny, the other with the rest of the kids, trying to piece together a life across two broken homes.

Or maybe we would have finally taken the risk and relinquished our rights, praying the state was bluffing about taking all of our children. Thank God we never had to find out.

My mom raised Manny for the next four years. She faced many of the same challenges I had, manipulation, defiance, disturbing behavior, but in a home without other children to protect, the danger felt less immediate.

It wasn't easy. But it was safer. Manny was always most dangerous when he had access to children. Without that dynamic, the threat wasn't gone, but it was contained. And for the first time in years, our home could breathe again.

Even into adulthood, he remained a master manipulator. In my mom's home, he could still twist the truth so convincingly, you'd doubt your own memory. He fooled everyone. Even my dad, a retired police officer trained in interrogation tactics, was taken in more times than he'd like to admit. Manny knew how to say the right things, mirror emotions, mimic accountability. But underneath, nothing had changed.

When he turned eighteen, he made a decision that shocked none of us: he chose to go live with his half-siblings and later his birth mother: the very family he'd been removed from as a child.

The cycle folded back in on itself.

With no rules, no boundaries, and no one telling him "no," he gave himself fully to the darkest parts of who he'd become. The safeguards were gone. And what remained was everything I had feared for so long.

Eventually, the truth became undeniable. He started a relationship with his older biological sister. Together, they had two children. The thought of that still takes my breath away of who he has become.

Today, he's in prison. The list of violent acts that led him there is long and harrowing.

He tried to choke his birth mother. He held a rifle to the stomach of the sister who was also the mother of his children. While on probation, he returned to his sister and beat her in the head with a tire iron and there is even more as to why he is in prison.

The shadows I had fought to keep at bay for years finally stepped into the light. Everything I tried so hard to protect my family from became someone else's nightmare. And part of me will always carry the guilt of ever letting him through our door.

I stayed so long because I believed I could help him.

Even in the darkest moments, when my body was worn down and my heart was unraveling, I held on to the hope that we could love him out of his pain. That if we just stayed steady, offering enough structure, enough safety, enough unconditional love, something would shift.

That the boy we saw glimpses of, the one who laughed, who played, who showed flickers of sweetness, might grow stronger with time.

I didn't want to give up. Giving up felt like failing. Failing him. Failing God.

When we adopted Manny, I believed it was a calling. That we were chosen for him, and he for us. So every time things got worse, I convinced myself we were just in the middle of the story. Not the end.

That healing was still coming. That redemption was just around the corner.

That if we could just hold on a little longer, things would finally turn.

And I knew, deep down, that if we let go and if we stopped fighting, his life was headed for pain. For destruction. I felt it in my bones. And I couldn't bear to be the one who opened the door to that path. I wanted to save him from it. I wanted to be the person who changed his story.

If we'd had the resources, I would've sent him to the best residential treatment center available: someplace with real therapeutic support. A place equipped to hold all of his brokenness without putting others at risk. But we weren't wealthy.

And the options available to families like ours, without money, were terrifying. They didn't help kids like Manny. They hardened them. They taught them to hide better, to manipulate deeper, or they surrounded them with other wounded children, feeding the very patterns we were trying to break.

I couldn't send him into that. Not while I still believed there was a chance.

So we stayed. We all stayed. Way past reason. Way past the point most families would have said "enough."

We stayed because we loved him. We stayed because we believed it was right. We stayed because we were desperate to believe that love could be enough.

But love wasn't enough.

Not this time.

And that truth still breaks something in me.

We lived for eight years in fear, and now his birth family he returned to are living in the wake of his destructive patterns. That's what haunts me most: that I couldn't stop the storm. I only moved it.

I wish we could have saved the little boy with the plastic bag of clothes who came through our door all those years ago.

Lessons in the Wilderness

* * *

One of the hardest moments in my journey was realizing I could not save Manny. For years, I believed that was the goal and the calling God had placed on my life. We had prayed for him, fought for him, protected him. I thought my obedience would be measured by his restoration.

So when it became clear that we had to let him go, it felt like failure not just as a parent, but as a believer. To walk away was to walk away from the very thing I thought God told me to do.

It took years for me to see it differently. Maybe the goal was never "save him." Maybe the goal was "give him the chance to be saved." And what he did with that chance was never mine to control.

God gives us free will, and He gives it to the people we love too. Even He, perfect in love and power, does not force anyone to choose Him. He simply offers the chance, again and again.

My part was obedience. God's part was the outcome.

I think of Paul's words in *1 Corinthians 3:6: "I planted the seed, Apollos watered it, but God has been making it grow."* We're not called to guarantee the harvest. We're called to plant, to water, to be faithful in the role we're given and then to release the results into God's hands.

If you've been holding onto a goal you feel you "failed" at, maybe it's worth asking: Did I fail? Or did I just misunderstand the assignment?

God isn't asking for perfect outcomes. He's asking for faithful obedience. And even when it looks like nothing grew, He may be working in ways you can't yet see.

And when that perceived failure feels overwhelming, remember this: obedience is costly, but we are not living for this moment. We are living for eternity. Our faithfulness today echoes far beyond what we can see.

"Therefore, my beloved brothers, be steadfast, immovable, always abounding in the work of the Lord, knowing that your labor in the Lord is not in vain."
— 1 Corinthians 15:58

* * *

Prayer:

Lord, when I feel like I've failed, remind me that my call is to faithful obedience, not perfect results. Help me to trust Your timing and Your ways, knowing You are the One who makes things grow. Strengthen my heart to keep planting and watering, even when I cannot see the harvest. May my faithfulness bring glory to You, now and for eternity. In Jesus' name, Amen.

17

A couple years after Manny left, Gio entered a new phase: girls, independence, and the slow pull of teenage rebellion. But rebellion looks different when the teen is still healing from trauma.

The stakes were higher. The wounds were deeper. For most teens, rebellion is about testing limits. For Gio, it was about survival strategies rising to the surface, defiance masking fear, secrecy covering shame, independence driven more by abandonment-avoidance than by growth.

And the hardest part? Just as we were finally starting to know the real Gio: the soft-hearted, funny, affectionate boy we had longed to reach, we were already beginning to lose him to adolescence.

It felt like we had only just begun rebuilding when another storm rolled in. If we had just a few more years of peace, I think it could have made a difference. But the healing was still fragile. The cement hadn't cured. And teenage rebellion hit like a hammer.

It started with small things.

Little acts of defiance. Testing boundaries. A sneaky sip of alcohol at a friend's house. Typical teen stuff on the surface, but with kids like Gio, nothing was ever just "typical."

Still, even in those early missteps, his tenderness would find a way through.

* * *

I remember the night he came to me, eyes red and voice shaking.

"I need to tell you something," he said, sitting in the passenger seat as I drove him home from baseball practice.

I looked over from the driver's seat. "Okay," I said gently. "What's going on?"

"I... I had a beer," he admitted. "Just one. At my friend's house. They didn't think it was a big deal."

I stayed quiet, letting him speak. I could tell there was more.

"But the second I drank it..." His voice cracked. He wiped at his eyes. "I remembered."

"Remembered what?" I asked, my heart already bracing.

He stared at the floor. "Everything." He paused gathering his strength before continuing. "Being little. Like... really little. I used to drink beer all the time. I didn't even think about it. I just grabbed the bottles from the fridge when I was thirsty. Nobody stopped me. It was just... normal."

His voice dropped to a whisper. "The taste brought it all back. Memories I had forgotten about."

He looked up at me, eyes full of saddness I had not seen in many years. "I never want to feel that again. I didn't know it would do that; I didn't know it would make me remember so much."

I reached over and took his hand in mine, feeling the weight of memory settle over the vehicle.

He was sad because something long-buried had resurfaced and he didn't want to go back there. Even in rebellion, Gio's heart was still soft. Still searching for safety. And still willing to come home.

But as peer pressure mounted, the struggles deepened. Sneaking out.

Lying. And then came the girlfriend.

That's when everything shifted.

Before her, Gio had mood swings, typical teenage turbulence, the kind we could weather. They didn't define him. He could get angry, sure. Withdrawn. But his heart always returned.

But after her, it was like something cracked open inside him. All the pain he had pushed down for years, loss, grief, confusion, and abandonment, rose to the surface, angry and wild.

It got worse.

He ran away once. Disappeared for days. No phone call. No text. No idea if he was alive or dead. And why?

It was all because we gave him an 11 p.m. curfew after his junior year spring formal. He was seventeen years old and we were trying to give him structure and guardrails instead of letting him plummet.

When he finally came home, we didn't yell. We didn't ground him for weeks or throw down ultimatums. We simply told him he couldn't stay in the apartment above the garage, the space he usually slept in, until trust was rebuilt. Just two weeks. Two weeks in the main house, under the same roof.

That was it, but even that felt like rejection to Gio.

When Gio learned that his consequence meant sleeping under the same roof as us for two weeks, something inside him snapped. Suddenly, he no longer wanted to live with us at all. He was seventeen, almost eighteen, and determined to make his own choices, no matter the cost.

We reached out to the local police for advice. They told us we could force Gio to stay home, but cautioned it might do more emotional harm than good. The police advised that as long as we knew where Gio was living and that he was safe, it might be best to let him decide where he wanted to be.

* * *

The day came when Gio showed up at our house to collect the last of his things. I didn't go outside. I stayed inside, pressed against the windowpane, watching quietly. I knew my presence would only stir his anger, and I wasn't sure either of us could handle that today.

Across the driveway, my husband met Gio.

Gio's face was flushed red with rage. His hands trembled as he shoved piles of clothes and boxes into his car. I could feel the storm in him: raw, chaotic, and painful. And all I could do was watch.

"You're not my father!" he screamed. "I hate you!" "All your sons hate you!"

There has never been a better, more loving and kind patient man than my husband. He is the best of fathers, but Gio aimed his insults well. Our older children were all raised in a house of chaos due to Manny and we had lost much of their hearts as a result.

Each accusation hit like a rock. And each time, I watched as my husband exuded so much love and self control. After each insult, my husband would reply with one of two things:

"I love you."

Or

"You'll always be my son."

That's all.

Even as Gio grabbed the last box, trembling with fury, my husband stood his ground; gentle but firm. "We're not kicking you out," he said. "This is your home. But if you live here, there have to be rules. You can't disappear for three days without telling us where you are. If you leave now, you're running away."

Gio turned to face him one last time. "FREEDOM!" he screamed at the top of his lungs from the driver's seat of his car.

* * *

Then tires screeched, gravel flew, and he was gone.

One day, he stopped by to grab some mail from the house. I met him at the door, held it out to him with a smile that I had to force through the pain. He snatched it from my hand without a word and turned to go.

"I love you," I called after him, trying desperately to recapture his heart.

He didn't turn around. Just kept walking.

And then he threw his words over his shoulder like a grenade. "@*!# you," he snarled back as he continue to walk away.

After that, the stories in our town started. We heard them through the grapevine. That we'd kicked him out. That he had nowhere to go. One version even claimed we made him sleep in a pantry.

Lies, but people believed them.

Not just strangers.

Friends.

People who had walked with us. Prayed with us. Sat at our table. People who had seen the inside of our home and the tears on our faces. And still, they chose the stories over our friendship. No calls. No questions. Just... silence.

And somehow, that silence cut deeper than Gio's words. Because it said: Maybe you really are the villain.

What hurt most wasn't the rebellion. It was the betrayal. I had loved Gio with everything I had. Fought for him. Cried over him. Dreamed for him. And in return, he handed out a narrative where I was the enemy and people believed it without asking me to speak.

I had only recently just come out of the isolation Manny forced me into and here I was, back in the same lonely place. Not because of what I'd done, but because of how easy it was for others to assume the worst.

What they didn't understand was this: even though Gio had healed more than Manny, he still lacked the deep attachment that might have anchored him differently. He loved us, yes, but when a child spends their early years in survival mode, love doesn't always come with trust. And without that internal connection, there's no inner compass pulling them back when they cross a line.

So much of our early relationship had been lost to chaos. By the time it settled enough for real bonding to begin, there just wasn't enough time.

Despite all the pain and difficult behaviors, I remained strong and still clung to hope that Gio would come back to our family. But one day, that fragile hope shattered in a way I never imagined. Gio, in the depth of his anger and pain, spoke of us with such bitterness and cruelty to a beloved family member.

He spoke to someone whose love and laughter had been a steady light in my life. That relationship, once a source of comfort and connection, was severed instantly. The silence that followed was deafening. That loss felt like a death. I had lost not just Gio, but also another family member and it felt like a part of my own soul had been ripped away.

I was left standing alone in the vastness of our country home, where the nearest neighbor was miles away and the quiet pressed in on me like a physical weight. The sky above was heavy and indifferent, a gray expanse that seemed to swallow all my cries. I stood in the middle of our lawn, looked up to the sky, and then, I screamed.

I screamed until my throat burned raw, until I was completely hoarse, as if every ounce of pain in my body was clawing to escape. The scream was more than words. It was the sound of a heart fracturing under unbearable grief. I sank to my knees on the cold earth, the roughness scraping my skin as the tears flowed without control, streaking down my face in desperate torrents.

For what felt like hours, I unleashed every broken piece of me into the vast silence breaking the silence with my cries. The anger at the seeming unfairness of the cost of adoption upon our family. The helplessness of loving someone who turned away in hate. The exhaustion from fighting battles no one else saw or understood. The loss of so much that I loved. The overwhelming loneliness that settled like a dark fog around me.

I screamed to the sky, "Why, God? Why this? Why us? Why did You call us to this journey if all it brings is heartbreak? Why is the love I poured out met with such rejection? Why did the dysfunction brought on from adoption cost me relationship with friends and other close family?"

I cried out the same questions over and over until my voice was raw and ragged. The questions pouring forth without hope for answers.

Sometimes I couldn't find words; all I could do was scream, a guttural sound that echoed my shattered spirit, a sound so full of anguish that it seemed to tear through the very air itself.

In that wilderness moment, the pain was not just sorrow. It was a storm of emotions: grief, shame, despair, anger, and a deep, aching confusion. It was feeling utterly invisible and utterly exposed, like my heart was a raw wound open to the world.

It was the ache of watching a child I loved more than life itself push me away, while everything I cherished was slipping through my fingers.

Eventually, with my body spent and my spirit battered, I dragged myself back inside. I saw his framed picture hanging on the wall. It held a place of honor I had given it years ago, a symbol of my hope and love. In that moment, it no longer held comfort. It was a painful reminder of the years filled mostly with struggle, disappointment, and darkness. My hands trembled as I took it down, and I carried it outside with a hammer in my grip.

Then, with every strike of the hammer against the frame and every shattered piece, I screamed again. The sound was raw, unfiltered pain. It was the culmination of fourteen years of relentless struggle, of hope met with heartbreak, of love poured into an abyss. Each crack of the hammer against the picture was a physical echo of the breaking inside me. I was broken, raw, exposed, and utterly shattered.

It was a moment where nothing felt sacred anymore, where the weight of it all crashed down, and I felt utterly lost in the wreckage of my own heart.

And yet, beneath that overwhelming hurt, there was a flicker, faint that was almost imperceptible, of a stubborn ember. It was the part of me that refused to give up completely, that somehow knew this was not the end of the story. But in that moment, that ember felt buried beneath a mountain of pain so heavy I feared I might never climb out.

That scream was not just an outburst; it was a lifeline thrown to the heavens above. It was a raw, human plea for mercy, for meaning, for a thread of hope to cling to amid the wreckage. It was one of the darkest nights I had ever known, and the silence that followed was so thick it felt like it might swallow me whole.

I lived in that place of despair and loss for over a year, but that's where Gio's story begins to diverge. As is often the case, God allows the dawn to break through after the darkest night.

One day, the fog lifted and Gio walked away from that unhealthy relationship. It was like blinders came off of his eyes overnight. Suddenly, he saw clearly, not just the damage she had done to him, but the pain he'd caused the people who loved him most.

He reached out to my husband first. His voice shaky on the phone, he admitted how blind he had been.

"I didn't see things for what they were," he said quietly. "I'm sorry." But he still wasn't ready to have a relationship with me.

My husband told him plainly, "Mom and I are a package deal."

A few days later, I sent Gio a message. "I love you," I wrote. "I'm sorry for any pain I caused. For anything I didn't handle well."

His reply came quicker than I expected. "Mom, can I take you to lunch for Mother's Day?" I felt excited like a school girl, but nervous because I didn't dare to hope yet that I had my son back.

The day arrived. He showed up at my door with a small bouquet of flowers: simple, but perfect. He was nervous, fumbling slightly as he handed them over and then drove us to a steakhouse.

We sat across from each other, sharing a meal that was about so much more than food. And as we talked, I felt like I was living the story of the parent of the prodigal son, right there in that restaurant. When I saw him, I gave him a small gift. Nothing fancy. Just a reminder that he was missed. Loved. Welcome.

It had been over a year since he'd been completely gone from our lives, but now, he was back and he came back with humility and love that filled every corner of my heart. Closer than ever before; closer even than the days when things were before the girlfriend.

He calls me now. He worries about me. He is kind. Compassionate. Everything a mother could hope her son would be. When all hope felt lost, he brought me flowers. And that day, everything changed.

Then he began building a real adult life. At eighteen, he became a police dispatcher: a job that requires steadiness and composure under pressure. He plans to serve in the military. He dreams of becoming a police officer. And he's doing the hard work to form healthier relationships: with us, with friends, with girlfriends.

It doesn't come naturally. He still hits emotional tripwires. But he is trying. His path is steeper than most, but he's walking it. He's choosing to grow. And that gives me hope.

Gio is not defined by his past. He's shaped by it, yes, but not imprisoned by it. Maybe that's what real healing looks like: not perfection, not a polished story, but a young man carrying the truth honestly, choosing love even when it costs him, and proving that redemption doesn't erase the pain; it grows from it.

Gio is not just learning to overcome, he's becoming someone entirely new: grounded, courageous, and deeply compassionate. The boy who once ran from his pain is now a man who chooses to stand in hard places with steady hands and a soft heart.

He sees the world differently because of what he's lived through and he shows up differently because of who he's chosen to become. He is not just surviving his story; he's leading it somewhere better. And that, to me, is the greatest kind of victory.

I feel honored everyday that I get to call him my son.

Lessons in the Wilderness

There's a story Jesus told that feels like it was made for moments like this: the story of the Prodigal Son. A son who left home full of anger and rebellion, who made choices that hurt those who loved him most. A son who hit rock bottom and then, against all odds, came home.

I remember the day Gio came back to us. After over a year of silence and pain, after words spoken in anger and distance that felt impossible to bridge, he showed up at our door. My heart was racing as I ran to him, arms wide open. I held him tight, the kind of hug that says, "You are still my son. You are still loved."

I gave him a small gift and a simple letter telling him how deeply I loved him, how I had never stopped hoping. Later, he took me to a Mother's Day lunch at a steakhouse. It was a quiet celebration, but to me, it felt monumental. Overnight, the boy who had been so full of hurt and hatred transformed into a son filled with love and devotion.

That day, I lived the prodigal story in a very real way. The pain of the wilderness, the wandering, the brokenness all led to this beautiful, dramatic and sudden moment of restoration. It reminded me that no matter how far someone has strayed, no matter how deep the hurt, the door home is always open.

If you're struggling with a wayward loved one, or feeling worn down by broken relationships, let this story encourage you: restoration is possible. It might not look the way you imagined, and it may take longer than you hoped. But love, grace, and forgiveness hold incredible power to heal what seems lost.

God's heart is always ready to welcome the lost home. His story is a promise that no one is beyond redemption, and no relationship is beyond repair. When we choose to love even in the darkest moments, we mirror the Father who waits with open arms.

Hold on to hope. Keep your heart open. Because miracles happen when least expected and the prodigal son's story isn't just a story; it can be your story too.

* * *

"But while he was still a long way off, his father saw him and was filled with compassion for him; he ran to his son, threw his arms around him and kissed him." — Luke 15:20

Prayer:

Lord, thank You for being the Father who never stops waiting, never stops loving, and always runs to welcome us home. Help me to hold onto hope and extend grace, even when the journey feels long and the wounds run deep. Restore what is broken and make way for miracles in the darkest places. In Jesus' name, Amen.

18

In the whirlwind of raising three trauma-scarred children alongside my biological kids, I felt like I was swimming upstream without a life jacket. Manny's volatility, Gio's fear-driven defiance, and Judy's fragile breakthroughs collided daily, while I still had diapers to change and meals to cook. I was overwhelmed and undertrained, floundering in waters deeper than I'd ever imagined. Even the most well-intentioned parent can drown without the right tools.

Looking back, I see how unequipped I was for what we faced. Judy's outbursts, Gio's deep-rooted fear, Manny's daily explosions: these were not minor misbehaviors. These were trauma responses, desperate cries from children who had seen too much and trusted too little.

And though I understood this in theory, in the moment, all I could feel was exhaustion. My patience wore thin. The truth is, their actions came from pain, not malice, but I often responded with frustration instead of compassion. Resources for parents navigating this kind of intensity were almost nonexistent.

One lifeline came from my mother. Nearly every day, I called her in tears, whispering, "I don't know how I'll survive fourteen more years of this." One day, she offered something that changed everything: "Let me take Judy for the summer. You need to breathe."

And breathe I did.

That summer was a turning point for me, for Judy, and for our entire family. Without the chaos of all three trauma-affected kids at once, I could finally focus on Gio. I wasn't drowning anymore. With space and calm, he began to bond more deeply with us. And Judy, removed from the overwhelming noise and emotional climate of our house, began to stabilize.

That one-on-one time with Grandma was a gift. Judy was seen. She had attention, quiet, consistency, and structure, but not at my expense. My mother respected my parenting choices and followed our household rules, so Judy didn't return viewing me as the "mean mom." Instead, the rules were reinforced in a different voice, under a gentler light.

With fewer kids around and no exposure to her biological brothers' intense behaviors, Judy wasn't constantly triggered. She wasn't feeding off their defiance or mimicking their chaos. In that peaceful environment, she began to learn how to regulate. She practiced emotional self-control not by force, but because the air finally allowed her lungs to expand. She was learning to breathe.

Meanwhile, I got a taste of something I hadn't felt in years: normal. With Manny in summer school and Judy away, our home felt... manageable. I could hear my own thoughts again. The younger kids laughed more. I could respond rather than react. For a moment, we felt like a regular family. That glimpse of peace became a lifeline. I wish I could say we stayed that way, but we didn't. Still, I now had a vision of what normal could look like and something to fight for.

When Judy came home, she was different. I cried on the phone to my mother, "You gave me my daughter back. Thank you." The rage was gone. The defiance, dulled. She was loving. Thoughtful. Calmer. We still had work to do, but the most destructive storms had passed.

From that experience, I learned something critical: adopting multiple children from trauma at the same time compounds the difficulty of their healing. They need space. They need one-on-one time. They need a chance to form healthy patterns without constantly being exposed to each other's pain.

If you're adopting a sibling group like I did, you must have structures in place to create separate healing environments. Trauma is contagious. If one child melts down and others are present, their nervous systems absorb that chaos. Separate the children when possible and remove the audience during a meltdown. It isn't punishment. It's protection.

And finally, know this: some healing takes more than consistency and love. It takes God.

I can't take credit for Judy's healing beyond offering rules, love, consistency, and getting her to church. Her transformation is something only God could do. There were moments, especially in those early years, where I was convinced nothing would ever change.

The first four years were devastating. Even when she improved at age six, there was still pain, still distance. Her salvation didn't fix everything overnight either. Giving her life to Christ opened the door, but she still had to walk the long road of restoration.

Healing is not linear. Redemption is not a straight path.

It's a roller coaster of steps forward and stumbles back. But slowly, the stumbles became smaller, and the steps longer. With time, the valleys grew shallower and the peaks higher.

Even the best outcomes, like Judy's, are hard-won. They are forged in prayer, in patience, in surrender. No child is beyond hope, but they must choose healing for themselves. God never forces transformation. They must partner with Him. They must want it.

All we can do is show them the way and pray they take it.

Parenting children emerging from deep trauma requires more than love. It demands humility, community, and the courage to ask for help. When my mother stepped in, I didn't just get a break, I got clarity, strength, and perspective. Sometimes, survival starts with stepping back just long enough to breathe, regroup, and prepare for the fight ahead.

Lessons in the Wilderness

* * *

When you've lived long seasons of survival and dysfunction, whether in your own heart or in your family, it's easy to lose sight of what "normal" looks like. Trauma and hardship can warp our expectations, making chaos feel familiar and peace feel foreign.

But God's Word reminds us that He came to give us life, and life to the fullest *(John 10:10)*. This abundant life includes peace, joy, and order even when the path to it is slow.

In the wilderness, the Israelites had to learn to trust God's timing and provision as they moved from survival toward a new normal. God gave them daily manna, enough for each day and no more, no less *(Exodus 16)*. They learned to receive God's provision bit by bit, trusting Him daily.

So can we.

Reclaiming normal isn't about perfect days or sudden miracles. It's about intentionally carving out small spaces of peace, joy, and health each day. It's choosing to let go of the chaos for just a moment and embrace God's order.

Paul encourages us:

"Do not conform to the pattern of this world, but be transformed by the renewing of your mind." (Romans 12:2)

Each day, find one small way to renew your mind and reclaim normal. When the storms rage and dysfunction feels overwhelming, hold onto this promise: God is making all things new *(Revelation 21:5)*. He is faithful to restore normalcy where brokenness has taken root.

Start small. Be consistent. Trust the process. Each day, carve out a little more space than the day before for Christ-centered peace, health, and normalcy to grow in your home and heart.

Prayer:

Father, in the midst of chaos and survival, help me to trust Your timing and provision. Teach me to reclaim normal, one small step at a time, by renewing my mind and embracing Your peace. Restore what is broken and make all things new in Your perfect way. In Jesus' name, Amen.

19

I survived. Barely, but I did. I raised a child who, by every clinical definition, was a psychopath. It nearly destroyed me physically, emotionally, spiritually. And yet, I did it.

People sometimes ask if I would do it again. That question is impossibly loaded. The truth? I would because adopting Manny meant adopting his brother and sister. Saying no to him would have meant leaving them all behind. And I couldn't do that. I couldn't turn my back on two children to avoid the storm that came with one.

His brother and sister are a priceless gift. I love them fiercely. I cannot imagine a world where I left them in foster care. But saying yes to them meant saying yes to Manny. And saying yes to Manny nearly destroyed my family.

If I could offer anything to someone considering adoption, it would be this: say yes, but go in with eyes wide open. Don't assume every story ends in healing and redemption. Some don't. Not every child can be loved into wholeness.

If you're adopting to give a child hope and a future they wouldn't otherwise have, that's the right reason. But if you're doing it to fill a void in your own life, and your story ends up like Manny's, that hole may only deepen. You could end up shattered.

Still, though I carry trauma from those years, I am not broken. I am changed and scarred, yes, but stronger. I know in my heart I gave that boy a chance he never would have had without me. And when I couldn't anymore, my mother stepped in and gave him yet another chance. What he did with those opportunities was his to decide. That part was never mine to control.

I showed up. I loved. I gave what I could. And when it wasn't enough, I let go. That has to be enough.

If I could go back, I wouldn't just love; I would be less naive. You can't always fix what trauma has fractured. Don't hand over full access to your world on day one. Trust must be earned, especially when other vulnerable children are in your home. By the time you see the danger, it might already be too late for someone else.

Also, don't isolate. Especially not when you're parenting a child from trauma. Isolation almost broke us. We had no mentors, no support system, no one to tell us, "It's okay to let go." I often wonder how different our life could have been if someone had seen what we couldn't and prayed when I no longer had the strength.

Isolation is a trap and too many parents raising trauma kids walk into it, thinking no one could possibly understand. But you need people. You need truth-tellers and grace-holders. Don't walk this alone.

We didn't step into isolation willingly. We were pushed by the relentless judgement of others. But still, I wish we had kept searching. I wish we hadn't let the disappointment convince us that no safe friend or trustworthy pastor existed. Maybe we couldn't avoid the loneliness, but I regret surrendering to it.

One more thing, if at all possible, do not adopt a child older than your youngest. Trauma sometimes shows up in predatory behaviors, and younger children are especially vulnerable. That kind of dynamic doesn't heal; it escalates. Your first job is to protect the children already in your home.

I truly believe if Manny had been placed in a home as an only child, or even as the youngest, his story might have been different. That was his one shot at healing. But the system insisted on keeping the siblings together, no matter the cost. In Manny's case, that cost was devastating. The placement he needed most was the one he never got.

And yet, this is not a story of regret. It's a story of clarity.

I did not fail Manny. I gave him everything I had. Others gave more. And in the end, his path is his to walk. What I've learned is this: love, while powerful, isn't always enough. Adoption is beautiful, but it can also be brutal. Choose it with eyes wide open.

Set boundaries. Use tools. Seek support. And protect the vulnerable.

I would do it again for the sake of the siblings and for the call I felt from God, but I would do it differently. Because now I know: hope must be paired with wisdom. Love must be guarded by truth. And mission must be carried with support. That's how you survive. That's how you stay whole.

There are stories where love wins and then there are stories like mine, where love was poured out daily and still couldn't change the outcome. I loved Manny with everything I had. I prayed. I fought. I stayed. And still, it ended in heartbreak. It changed all of us forever.

But where my love reached its limits, God did not.

He carried me through nights I thought I wouldn't survive. He stayed when I was ready to give up. His strength met me when mine collapsed. I didn't come out unscarred, but I came out held.

Because in the end, our job isn't always to fix. Sometimes, it's simply to obey. And when obedience breaks your heart, God is still enough.

Looking back now, I can see the miracles more clearly. At the time, it felt like everything was falling apart, but God was holding every shattered piece in His hands. He saved me. He saved my children.

I didn't survive because I'm strong. I survived because He is.

He was the steady whisper in the storm, the anchor in the chaos. And now, years later, I see His fingerprints on every page of our story.

* * *

This wasn't the ending I prayed for, but it was the one God carried me through. And that is enough.

Lessons in the Wilderness

"Let us not become weary in doing good, for at the proper time we will reap a harvest if we do not give up." — Galatians 6:9

Sometimes, doing the right thing feels like an uphill battle that never ends. Raising children with trauma, loving when love doesn't seem to change anything, standing firm when others walk away, it can wear down even the strongest heart.

You may feel like you've given everything and yet the breakthrough never comes. The pain still lingers. The chaos still rages. And the harvest seems far away, if it's even coming at all.

But God's promise is clear: perseverance matters. Every moment you choose to love, protect, and obey, even when it's exhausting and thankless, is not wasted.

It might seem like I didn't follow this very advice with Manny. At times, it felt like I was growing weary to the point of breaking. But not growing weary in doing good also means knowing when to set healthy boundaries and when to shift the focus of your good. Sometimes, loving well means stepping back, saying "enough," and protecting the vulnerable in your care.

Perseverance is not blind endurance. It is wise, discerning, and sometimes courageous enough to say, "This is how I will love now." It's in this balance that our obedience honors both God's heart and the wellbeing of those around us.

This verse reminds us that our faithfulness is more important than instant results. Sometimes the reward is invisible, hidden beneath the surface, growing slowly in ways we can't yet see.

Sometimes the reward isn't a story of a child redeemed here on earth. Sometimes the reward is the one we receive in heaven for every sacrifice made, every moment spent offering love and a chance at redemption, even if that love was rejected. God sees those acts of faithfulness, and He honors them eternally.

It's okay to be tired. It's okay to feel worn down. But don't quit. Because God's timetable is perfect, and His rewards are eternal.

Remember the story of Joseph, sold into slavery and thrown into prison, yet he never gave up. Years later, God elevated him to save nations. Your story might feel like a wilderness season right now, but the reward is coming.

Hold fast to the truth: your good work for the Lord matters. Your sacrifices are not in vain. God is working in ways you cannot see.

Keep doing good, keep trusting, keep loving.

Prayer:

Lord, when I grow weary, remind me that my faithfulness matters, even when I can't see the fruit. Help me to love wisely and persevere with courage, trusting Your perfect timing and eternal rewards. Strengthen my heart and renew my hope today. In Jesus' name, Amen.

20

Gio represents the good side of adoption. Not perfect; far from it. His journey was long and hard, and for many years, I wasn't sure we were succeeding at all. Until he became an adult, I honestly wondered if we had failed again. Failed to redeem his story; failed to reach his heart.

Gio wasn't cruel like Manny, but he didn't seem to love us either. For a long time, I wrestled with that painful question: What was the point of adoption if every child we gave our lives to grew up to resent us?

I had to remind myself often: we didn't adopt them so they would love us. We adopted them so they would be loved. We adopted them to give them a chance at life they never would have had otherwise. To show them the love of Jesus. To give them a family, even if they didn't know how to receive it. Those truths became anchors on the darkest days with Gio, especially when all I could feel from him was rejection or hatred. I repeated them to myself like a lifeline, because without them, I might've let despair take root.

I truly thought he would never accept us as Mom and Dad. I had resigned myself to that reality... grieved it, even. But then, we had what I can only call a miracle. He didn't just tolerate us in his life, he embraced us as his parents. The very thing I had once believed impossible actually happened. I never stopped praying for Gio, but I did stop believing. I lost faith that anything would ever change. But somehow, buried beneath all that doubt, there was still a flicker of hope. I must have believed, deep down, that God could do the impossible because I never stopped praying. And God did.

* * *

Gio's instinct to protect himself through physicality has transformed in his adult years. He's no longer reactive or aggressive unless it's to defend someone else. But his body still tells a story. Strong, muscular, and always alert, he carries himself like a quiet warning: Don't try to hurt me or anyone I love. His very presence speaks what words no longer need to; he's not the scared little boy anymore. He's a man who's prepared to stand his ground, not out of anger, but out of hard-won strength.

That strength, both physical and emotional, is how Gio has coped with the powerlessness he felt in his younger years. Building his body became a way to reclaim a sense of control over a life that once left him vulnerable.

It's a healthier coping mechanism than many others he could have chosen, but it didn't happen overnight. It took time, maturity, and countless conversations with us about what true strength looks like. We helped him understand when it's right to stand firm and when it's just as brave to walk away.

In the same vein as building his physical strength, Gio has also worked hard to develop healthier coping mechanisms around food. What once was a battleground of impulse and fear has slowly become a space of discipline and awareness.

I think it helped when I gently showed him pictures of his birth family, not to shame, but to give him perspective. He saw the generational pattern of morbid obesity, the health consequences, the lack of care. He didn't want that for himself. In his own words, "I've already had to survive too much. I don't want my body to be another thing I have to fight." That realization became a turning point.

There were also important conversations when Manny moved back in with his birth family. I remember the day Manny left, I gently warned him: "You're going to have to work hard to stay healthy around your birth family. There are some really unhealthy habits in that home." He was furious with me for saying it. But I shared that moment with Gio, not to gossip, but to help him understand the patterns he might one day face himself.

* * *

Sure enough, within just a couple of months, Manny went from being fit and active to severely overweight. When Gio saw the photos of that change, it hit him hard. He saw for himself that there was a family dynamic pulling toward unhealthiness physically, emotionally, and even spiritually. And unlike Manny, Gio decided to fight against it.

Gio truly wanted a different outcome for himself and he earned it. Today, I'd even say he's healthier than any of us, carefully watching what he eats and staying committed to caring for his body. It's more than just fitness for him; it's ownership over his life, over what goes into him, and who he becomes.

One of the biggest lessons we learned through Gio's journey is this: if you adopt sibling groups, you must be intentional about protecting them from forming unhealthy trauma bonds with each other. I look back and deeply wish we had been able to keep Gio away from Manny more often.

We truly did everything we could, but we were financially strapped, and the two boys had to share a room in the very beginning. That dynamic shaped so much of what followed. I say this to every prospective adoptive parent now: 'don't adopt if you can't give each child their own space. Separate rooms aren't a luxury in adoption; they're a necessity for healing.'

Additionally, Gio and his biological sister shared a bond that, while understandable, ultimately hindered his ability to connect with the rest of the family. For a long time, Gio wouldn't play with or even engage much with the other children in the home. Only her.

At the time, I let it happen. I thought he was just finding comfort in what he knew. But looking back, I wish I had intervened earlier. I should have gently required more time where Gio interacted with his other siblings, encouraged activities that built trust and connection across the whole family and not just within the biological bond.

Letting him stay only in that one safe zone delayed his ability to see us as his family too. If I could go back, I would have been far more intentional about helping him form new, healthier attachments not just to us, but to all his siblings.

Even his lack of love for us in those early years, I gave him space. I thought I was respecting his boundaries and that forcing connection would backfire. But looking back, I should have pushed in. I should have hugged him more, even when he stood there stiff as a board.

I told him I loved him often, but I wish I had done more to chip away at those walls instead of waiting for them to fall on their own. Because they don't. Not with kids like Gio. The walls stay unless someone is brave enough to keep knocking, over and over, with tenderness and persistence.

I still wonder about the therapist's early suspicion of bipolar disorder. For a time, I believed it. The mood swings were intense. The lows were frightening. But whether that label was wrong or Gio simply overcame what once seemed inevitable, I don't know.

What I do know is that now, today, he's winning. He still has his lows, but they no longer define him. His emotions don't hijack his whole life. He battles for joy, and most days, he wins.

This took years of intentional help from us. Before medication was even on the table, we worked tirelessly with Gio on how to regulate his emotions. We coached him through meltdowns, talked him down from panic, helped him name feelings he didn't yet understand. It wasn't quick or easy, but it was consistent. And somewhere along the way, things shifted.

Whether it was a miracle, a misdiagnosis, or the sheer fruit of his determination, I can say with confidence: I do not believe Gio is bipolar. I think in a different life, with different support, and a different environment, mental illness might have taken hold. He had every vulnerability. But that is not his story anymore. He rewrote it. God rewrote it.

The bad hygiene and bathroom habits Gio once had are long gone. So far gone, in fact, that it's hard to believe they were ever part of his story. In yet another example of how he became the opposite of who he was as a child, Gio swung to the other extreme and, for a season, bordered on being a germaphobe.

Anything remotely gross or unhygienic, he avoided like the plague. This same boy who once struggled so deeply with hygiene that he soiled vents and wiped with curtains now keeps himself and his surroundings spotless. Of all my children, he is the most particular about cleanliness.

It's almost poetic: the child who once lived in filth now chooses order, hygiene, and control over his space. It's like he reclaimed something that was stolen from him.

This isn't a memoir for the sake of memoir. This is a tool. A tool to help other adoptive families feel less alone. A tool to help friends, churches, and communities understand what adoption really asks of a family, and how easily misunderstanding can turn into judgment instead of support.

There's no way to fully capture what life was like during those years with Manny in our home or the ripple effect it had on all the children, especially Gio. You've read these stories one at a time, but I lived them all at once.

Three adopted children carrying their own storms and colliding with each of their extreme behaviors in our home day after day, sometimes hour after hour. The constant state of being worn thin left me with little reserve, and it cost Gio the one thing he needed most from me: my patience with his choices and my undivided attention.

And within that reality, Gio was one of the quiet casualties of my constant need to survive and to help the others survive the presence of Manny, a literal psychopath, living under our roof.

Gio had inner battles I never knew about until he was an adult, as did some of my biological children. That is a pain I can never make right as a mother. I can never undo that I was so focused on our survival that I missed things, subtle signs of hidden struggles, that a mother should have seen.

That is a guilt I will carry with me to my grave. Because I opened up my home to children in need, I also opened the door to a level of pain and suffering that could have been avoided, or at least addressed and tended to, if I hadn't been so constantly distracted by the chaos and danger Manny brought.

Our most basic job as parents is to keep our children safe. I failed them by allowing Manny in our home and by not removing him sooner. That failure is mine alone. I pray that my children can forgive me for that. I pray that someday the good we tried to do can stand tall enough to help them see our hearts, even in our mistakes.

Once Manny was in our home, there was no undoing it, but that one decision forever changed our family for the worse.

Gio, I'm sorry I missed that you were hurting and needed my help. I thought I was keeping you safe, but I see now how much I missed. I was looking at the danger in front of me, and I didn't notice the quiet suffering beside me. You needed me, and I wasn't there in the way I should have been.

Gio and his sister, and my biological children, are incredible human beings. They have shown me so much grace and have forgiven me for my many shortcomings as a mother. There is no handbook on how to keep your family safe when a literal psychopath lives under your roof.

There's no guide for how to stay soft and calm when every day feels like a battle between life and death, for almost a decade. I became a yelling mom. I became a tired mom. I became a surviving mom. And I mourn the gentler mother I wanted to be, the one they deserved.

Now that Manny is gone, I am back to who I was before Manny. It took me a couple years to get here, but I'm back. I'm calm. I'm happy. I lavish love on my kids again. I still have some PTSD and can be triggered by certain conversations or actions, but overall, I'm back to being a fully functioning, healthy mom. The kind of mom my kids deserve.

Unfortunately, I didn't regain my peace until after Gio was out of the home. He didn't get to experience this version of me. He knew the highly stressed, exhausted mom. The one who was trying desperately to hold everything together.

But even in that season of survival, there were moments. Moments of deep talks. Of laughter. Of love. Of connection that was real. And so when he ran away, I prayed he would come back. I hoped, but if I'm honest, I didn't believe he ever would.

Gio's first five years were nothing but trauma, and then after that, though he had a home filled with love, it was also sometimes filled with chaos, stress, and dysfunction because of Manny. Gio's childhood was marked by moments of calm, but peace was never constant and because of that, I truly didn't think he would come back. But he did.

He returned with love in his heart for our family, with gratitude, with a maturity and depth that honestly took my breath away. He became an amazing human being. Not just in spite of everything he went through, but maybe even because of how he chose to rise above it.

One huge takeaway from Gio's story is this: don't stop believing in your adopted child's redemption story. Even when it feels hopeless. Even when the pain has gone on too long. Even when the walls feel permanent.

When the walls feel permanent, keep loving anyway. When faith runs dry, whisper a prayer anyway. God is still in the business of impossible things.

This shows that the adopted child has to want to break the cycles they were born into. When Gio didn't want to break those cycles, he absolutely did not. He wasn't evil or bad, but he was stuck in a pattern that had been ingrained in him from birth.

For a long time, he simply lived out what had always been normal for him. But once his eyes were opened to the generational curses he was born into, he fought. He fought hard to break free from them.

He still has some growing to do, as we all do, but he is on a path toward becoming someone entirely different from who he was once destined to become. He has changed his future. He has changed the future of his children. He is living proof that redemption is possible.

* * *

Gio's story reminds me that while love, structure, and safety are essential, healing only happens when the child chooses it for themselves. We couldn't make that choice for him, but we stayed steady until he was ready. And when he was, he didn't run away. He ran toward life.

That's what makes all the heartbreak worth telling. Gio chose a different future and in doing so, he has already changed generations. He is not the boy he once was. He's a man who stood at the edge of what he came from and walked a different way.

Lessons in the Wilderness

"For we do not wrestle against flesh and blood, but against the rulers, against the authorities, against the cosmic powers over this present darkness..."
— *Ephesians 6:12*

If you are in a wilderness season right now, whether it's parenting trauma-affected children, walking through loss, or facing overwhelming challenges, know this: you are not just battling circumstances or people. You are in a spiritual war.

Sometimes the fight feels exhausting because we are only wrestling in the natural, in what we can see or control. But Scripture reveals the real enemy is spiritual, working through fear, anger, division, and chaos.

I want to share a hard lesson I learned through raising Gio and Manny. Many times, when worship music would come on, instead of peace filling our home, their behavior got worse. I got frustrated and turned the music off eager for a quick remedy to stop the chaos.

Looking back, I realize those moments were spiritual attacks. Worshiping Jesus stirred something in the spirit realm, and the enemy didn't want to lose ground. Instead of turning off worship, I should have turned it UP. I should have prayed, rebuked the devil, and declared God's presence over the chaos.

If you're in your own wilderness season right now, don't be unaware of the spiritual battle around you. When things feel hardest, lean into worship, prayer, and the Word. Rebuke the enemy with authority. Speak life over your home, your children, your heart.

Remember the armor God gives you—truth, righteousness, peace, faith, and salvation *(Ephesians 6:14-17)*. Use it. Don't shrink back. The enemy fears the name of Jesus and the power of your worship.

This wilderness is not just a struggle; it's a battlefield.

Be alert. Be prayerful. Be bold.

God is with you. His Spirit is your greatest weapon.

Prayer:
Jesus, I recognize the spiritual battle raging in my life and my home. Help me to fight not with frustration or fear, but with worship, the Word, and prayer. Give me courage to rebuke the enemy and declare Your peace and protection. Let my worship be a powerful weapon that pushes back darkness. I stand firm in Your victory. In Your name, Amen.

21

Some seeds take decades to bloom. Some may never bloom where we can see. But if I've learned anything, it's this: obedience is still worth it, even when the fruit takes a lifetime to grow.

The story of Manny, Gio, and Judy doesn't offer easy answers. But it does offer truth… truth about adoption. Real adoption. The kind that is complicated, costly, and full of both heartbreak and wholeness. It wrecks you and rebuilds you. It teaches you what love really costs.

When we first said yes, I had no idea what that "yes" would demand. I thought love would be enough. That time would heal. That effort would bring reward. But obedience to God doesn't guarantee ease; it only guarantees His presence on the road. And still, even after everything, I would say yes again.

Sometimes, a child is born into the worst imaginable circumstances: no hope, no future, no reason to believe life could ever be good. And then, by grace, they come into your home. You offer them a future they never dreamed possible. And in return, you receive a gift far greater than you gave.

You gain a daughter who becomes your pride and joy. A child who grows into your best friend. A soul so radiant and resilient she becomes everything a child should be.

That is our Judy.

* * *

She is the reason adoption is worth it. For every Judy out there waiting for a home, for hope, for someone to believe in them I would say yes all over again. Even knowing the pain. Even carrying the scars. Even with the impact it had on my biological children.

Because love like hers doesn't just fill a home. It transforms it.

But not every adoption story ends with a Judy.

I need to say that honestly.

Gio's story, so much harder, so much more complicated, was still worth it. His journey didn't end in the kind of resolution I once prayed for. But it wasn't without redemption.

There were moments. Glimpses of light through the cracks in his hardened defenses. Even though his story is marked by struggle, it's not only pain. His life was spared. He was given a chance to become more than what he came from. And while I didn't get joy-filled memories during his teen years, I know adoption changed him. I know love was planted deep, even if it took years to take root.

Adoption isn't about feeling loved in return. It's not about emotional reward. I didn't feel that from Gio, not until his adult years. But adoption was never about what we'd receive. It was about giving a child a hope and a future they might never have known. It was about loving them when they didn't know how to accept it. Gio's story took longer to bloom. But it was never a waste.

Still, if you are truly called to adopt, it is worth it. Not because it's easy. Not because it's fair. But because it can alter the entire trajectory of a life.

Adoption left permanent marks on our family. It caused wounds I'll grieve for the rest of my life. And yet, I know I made a difference in three lives. I gave them a future they wouldn't have had without us. And that has to be enough.

Obedience to God was costly. No one promised it wouldn't be. But we're not living for comfort; we're living for eternity. What I did for those three children, and what it cost me, matters in the eyes of heaven. I believe that with every fiber of my being.

Still, I never could have imagined just how high the cost would be.

If I had known then what I know now: how much pain it would cause, how deeply it would wound my biological children, I would have entered this journey differently. I would have come armed with more training, more resources, more safeguards. I would have done so many things differently.

And if I had known then what I know now...I wouldn't have adopted Manny as long as I could still adopt Judy and Gio.

Not because he wasn't worthy of love. But because the depth of his trauma was more than I could handle. Sometimes, a child's wounds are so deep that love alone can't reach them, not in this life.

But that's the thing about obedience: it doesn't come with guarantees. God didn't ask me to say yes because the outcome was assured. He asked me to rescue the children He placed before me. The result? That was always His to hold.

Now that our adoption journey is behind us and all three of our children are adults, I can look back with clarity. Yes, parts of our family were broken along the way. Yes, the cost was steep. But I've also seen miracles. Real ones. I've seen God begin to heal what was shattered. I've seen redemption where there once was only ruin.

Even now, even knowing everything, I would do it again.

Don't let the horror stories keep you from what God is asking of you. Adoption is not safe. It is rarely easy. But for some children, it's the only door to hope. And for those who are called, obedience is always worth the cost.

But if you're not called to adopt, that's okay. Not everyone is. That's not a failure of compassion. It's just reality. But Scripture is clear: everyone is called to care for the widow and the orphan in their distress.

* * *

That care doesn't always look like bringing a child into your home. Sometimes it looks like showing up for the family who did. It looks like offering respite, or bringing a meal, or sending a note that says, "You're not alone." It looks like listening without judgment. Stepping into someone else's storm and helping them stay afloat.

Loving the orphan also means loving the weary, messy families who said yes to them. Show up. Offer grace. Be kind. Your presence might be the thing that helps them keep going.

We are all called to adoption in some way. Maybe not into our homes, but into our hearts. Into the messy, holy work of lifting up the vulnerable. Some are called to adopt. Others are called to support, to carry burdens, to link arms with those in the thick of it.

"Pure and undefiled religion before God the Father is this: to care for orphans and widows in their distress." (James 1:27)

That care will look different for each of us. But the call is the same: love sacrificially. Stand in the gap. Say yes to the hard, holy work of lifting up the brokenhearted.

If I've learned anything, it's this: obedience is always worth it, even when it costs everything.

Manny may never become the son I hoped for. But we said yes. Gio's healing came slowly and unevenly, but it came. And Judy? She is living proof that love can raise what was dead.

I didn't save them all.

But I was faithful.

We were faithful.

And that is enough.

In the end, this isn't just a story about adoption. It's about surrender. It's about trusting that when we offer God our yes, He can turn it into a miracle, even if it breaks us along the way.

May your yes, wherever it leads and whatever the cost, become someone else's miracle.

So if you're reading this, whether you're deep in the struggle, just beginning the journey, or unsure if you can take that next step, know this: God is faithful. The road may be steep and the outcome uncertain, but obedience to Him is never wasted.

His Word does not return void. Even when you can't see the fruit, He is working beneath the surface. And one day, maybe here or maybe in eternity, you will see how your "yes" was part of someone else's redemption story.

Love doesn't always look like victory here on earth. Sometimes it looks like perseverance. Sometimes it looks like tears. But when offered to God, even the broken pieces become holy. Even the hardest stories can become altars of His grace.

So say yes. Not because it's easy, but because He is worthy. And because on the other side of that yes, there just might be a miracle waiting.

Lessons in the Wilderness

"The LORD is faithful to all his promises and loving toward all he has made." — Psalm 145:13b

The journey of adoption, parenting, or any hard calling can feel like wandering in a wilderness — long, uncertain, and full of challenges. Like the Israelites who spent forty years in the desert before entering the Promised Land, you may wonder if your faithfulness is making a difference. But here is a timeless truth: God is faithful, and your yes today can become someone else's miracle tomorrow.

Think of Esther. When she said yes to the terrifying call to stand before the king unbidden, she risked her life. Yet her obedience became the means of salvation for her entire people. Her courage planted a seed of deliverance that echoes through history. Esther's yes was about faith in God's plan and a willingness to be used for something greater than herself.

Or consider Joseph, who endured betrayal, slavery, and imprisonment. His steadfastness and faithfulness led him to a place where he could save entire nations from famine. Joseph's long, painful journey in the wilderness was not wasted. His yes, even in hardship, became a lifeline for his family and many others.

Your story may not look like Esther's or Joseph's, but your yes matters just the same. The sacrifices, the prayers, the love you pour out, even when it's costly and confusing, are never wasted. God sees every act of faithfulness and will use it in ways you can't yet imagine.

Sometimes, the fruit of your obedience won't be fully visible in this life. Maybe the child you prayed for isn't yet healed. Maybe the family is still walking through storms. But your yes is part of a greater story of redemption and grace.

God is weaving your faithfulness into a tapestry far beyond what you see. And one day, maybe here on earth, or maybe in eternity, your yes will be recognized as a miracle to someone else.

"Therefore, my dear brothers and sisters, stand firm. Let nothing move you. Always give yourselves fully to the work of the Lord, because you know that your labor in the Lord is not in vain." — *1 Corinthians 15:58*

God is faithful. Your yes is powerful. Keep saying yes, trusting that the miracles you long to see are already in motion.

Prayer:

Father, thank You for Your unfailing faithfulness. When the wilderness feels long and the journey uncertain, help me to stand firm in obedience and trust. Use my yes, even when it feels small or costly, to bring about Your miracles in ways I cannot see. Strengthen my faith and remind me that my labor for You is never in vain. In Jesus' name, Amen.

22

This is simply our story. While some have faced more difficult adoption journeys, and others far smoother ones, what we experienced is not unusual as it may seem. In fact, much of what we endured is common among families who adopt older children.

I know this story will stir strong reactions. Some will wonder why I didn't act sooner or why I let Manny stay as long as I did. Others will say I never should have let him go at all; that a mother should never give up on her child.

The truth is, we did the best we could with what we had. There are no simple answers when you're living inside the storm. The choice to say, "You can no longer live in this home," is one of the most agonizing a parent can face. It's not about giving up. It's about trying to survive. It's about protecting the children who are still able to heal, even when one is too broken to stay.

This wasn't a failure of love. It was a limit of what love alone could do.

That gut-wrenching decision is something no one can truly understand unless they've lived it.

Because of that choice, my family is whole again. We are happy. My older children, those who bore the weight of my own pain as I fought to protect them from Manny, will likely carry some scars from a childhood where their mother was stretched beyond what any parent should endure. I wasn't always the mother they deserved, because survival took all my focus.

That is the hardest part. Seeing my older children struggle in their adult life because of the chaos Manny brought into our home for so many years. That guilt can consume me if I let it, but I have to let it go and trust God with their stories.

But my younger children have a different story. Our home has returned to what it once was: a place filled with joy, peace, and freedom from dysfunction. Life, for the first time in a long time, feels good.

And through it all, I survived.

But more than that, I was changed. I discovered strength I didn't know I had, faith that held firm when everything else shook, and a kind of love that bled, healed, and endured. Raising Manny didn't just test me, it transformed me.

This story isn't just one of survival. It's a story of redemption. Of restoration. Of God doing what only He can do, bringing beauty from ashes.

And as I look around this home once again filled with laughter, I don't just feel relief. I feel victory.

I didn't just survive raising Manny.

By God's grace… I overcame.

Stephanie Parker is a wife, mom, and storyteller whose life is shaped by faith, family, and the fierce love it takes to walk through hard seasons together. She met her husband, Adam, when they were just teenagers, and for more than 25 years they've been building a life side by side, one marked by deep commitment and the everyday choice to love well.

As the mother of eight children, three adopted from foster care, Stephanie has lived the joys and heartbreaks of adoption in real time. She knows what it's like to wrestle with trauma, fight for attachment, and cling to hope when the road feels impossibly long.

Through her writing and speaking, Stephanie invites adoptive parents into honest conversations about healing, perseverance, and the God who meets us in the middle of the mess. At home, you'll find her and Adam in the thick of family life, cheering for their kids, laughing in the kitchen, praying through the hard days, and learning that love is most powerful when it's tested.

www.ingramcontent.com/pod-product-compliance
Lightning Source LLC
LaVergne TN
LVHW051555080426
835510LV00020B/2991